DEVELOPING EFFECTIVE TRAINING SKILLS
Second edition

Latest titles in the McGraw-Hill Training Series

Details of these and other titles in the series are available from:

The Product Manager, Professional Books, McGraw-Hill Book Company Europe,
Shoppenhangers Road, Maidenhead, Berkshire SL6 2QL, United Kingdom
Tel: 01628 23432 Fax: 01628 770224

Developing effective training skills

A practical guide to designing and delivering group training

Second edition

Tony Pont

McGRAW-HILL BOOK COMPANY

London · New York · St Louis · San Francisco · Auckland
Bogotá · Caracas · Lisbon · Madrid · Mexico · Milan
Montreal · New Delhi · Panama · Paris · San Juan · São Paulo
Singapore · Sydney · Tokyo · Toronto

Published by
McGRAW-HILL Book Company Europe
Shoppenhangers Road, Maidenhead, Berkshire, SL6 2QL, England
Telephone: 01628 23432
Fax: 01628 770224

British Library Cataloguing in Publication Data
Pont, Tony
    Developing effective training skills : a practical guide to
    designing and delivering group training. – 2nd ed. –
    (McGraw-Hill training series)
    1. Employees – Training of 2. Employee training personnel –
    Training of
    I. Title
    658.3'124'04

ISBN 0-07-709143-4

Library of Congress Cataloging-in-Publication Data
Pont, Tony
    Developing effective training skills : a practical guide to
    designing and delivering group training / Tony Pont. – 2nd ed.
        p.   cm.
    Includes bibliographical references and index.
    ISBN 0-07-709143-4 (pbk. : alk. paper)
    1. Employees–Training of.   I. Title.
    HF5549.5.T7P615   1996
    658.3'124–dc20   95-51295
                                                                               CIP

McGraw-Hill
A Division of The **McGraw·Hill** Companies

12345 CUP 99876

Typeset by BookEns Limited, Royston, Herts
and printed and bound in Great Britain at the University Press, Cambridge
Printed on permanent paper in compliance with ISO Standard 9706

For Leslie Rupert,
who would have appreciated the effort

Contents

Series preface

Training and development are now firmly centre stage in most organizations, if not all. Nothing unusual in that—for some organizations. They have always seen training and development as part of the heart of their businesses—but more and more must see it that same way.

The demographic trends through the 1990s will inject into the marketplace severe competition for good people who will need good training. Young people without conventional qualifications, skilled workers in redundant crafts, people out of work, women wishing to return to work—all will require excellent training to fit them to meet the job demands of the 1990s and beyond.

But excellent training does not spring from what we have done well in the past. T&D specialists are in a new ball game. 'Maintenance' training—training to keep up skill levels to do what we have always done—will be less in demand. Rather, organization, work and market change training are now much more important and will remain so for some time. Changing organizations and people is no easy task, requiring special skills and expertise which, sadly, many T&D specialists do not possess.

To work as a 'change' specialist requires us to get to centre stage—to the heart of the company's business. This means we have to ask about future goals and strategies, and even be involved in their development, at least as far as T&D policies are concerned.

This demands excellent communication skills, political expertise, negotiating ability, diagnostic skills—indeed, all the skills a good internal consultant requires.

The implications for T&D specialists are considerable. It is not enough merely to be skilled in the basics of training, we must also begin to act like business people and to think in business terms and talk the language of business. We must be able to resource training not just from within but by using the vast array of external resources. We must be able to manage our activities as well as any other manager. We must share in the creation and communication of the company's vision. We must never let the goals of the company out of our sight.

In short, we may have to grow and change with the business. It will be hard. We shall have to demonstrate not only relevance but also value for money and achievement of results. We shall be our own boss, as accountable for results as any other line manager, and we shall have to deal with fewer internal resources.

The challenge is on, as many T&D specialists have demonstrated to me over the past few years. We need to be capable of meeting that challenge. This is why McGraw-Hill Book Company Europe have planned and launched this major new training series—to help us meet that challenge.

The series covers all aspects of T&D and provides the knowledge base from which we can develop plans to meet the challenge. They are practical books for the professional person. They are a starting point for planning our journey into the twenty-first century.

Use them well. Don't just read them. Highlight key ideas, thoughts, action pointers or whatever, and have a go at doing something with them. Through experimentation we evolve; through stagnation we die.

I know that all the authors in the McGraw-Hill Training Series would want me to wish you good luck. Have a great journey into the twenty-first century.

ROGER BENNETT
Series Editor

About the series editor

Roger Bennett has over 20 years' experience in training, management education, research and consulting. He has long been involved with trainer training and trainer effectiveness. He has carried out research into trainer effectiveness, and conducted workshops, seminars and conferences on the subject around the world. He has written extensively on the subject including the book *Improving Trainer Effectiveness*, Gower. His work has taken him all over the world and has involved directors of companies as well as managers and trainers.

Dr Bennett has worked in engineering, several business schools (including the International Management Centre, where he launched the UK's first masters degree in T&D), and has been a board director of two companies. He is the editor of the *Journal of European Industrial Training* and was series editor of the ITD's *Get In There* workbook and video package for the managers of training departments. He now runs his own business called The Management Development Consultancy.

About the author

Dr Tony Pont is a management training and development consultant and a graduate of the Universities of Leeds and Bradford.

He has held appointments in Further and Higher Education and in industry. In 1982 he obtained a Fulbright Exchange Award to the USA.

He has extensive international experience in Europe, USA and SE Asia having undertaken assignments with clients in the public sector, pharmaceuticals, oil and gas, construction, automobiles, retailing and financial services. He has acted as a consultant to the Institute of Management, is a visiting faculty member at three of the UK's leading business schools working on qualification programmes including the MBA, and is a Director of Heyford Associates, a HRD consultancy based in Northamptonshire.

He is married and lives near Northampton with his wife and two children.

Preface

George Bernard Shaw once wrote 'He who can, does. He who cannot, teaches.' For those who have tried, there is a sudden realization that teaching is not as easy as first thought. It is not merely a question of standing in front of an audience and casting one's pearls.

For those who have been involved in the teaching of adults there is an immediate realization of the difficulty of this challenge. At the same time there is a quick understanding of the enormous satisfaction and stimulation that one can enjoy when the process is carried out professionally.

In today's rapidly changing world the need for training is of greater importance. The days when an individual learned skills under apprenticeship, articles, professional training, etc., that were to equip that individual with a job for life have long since gone. Learning is now a lifelong process and is necessary not just for personal growth and development, but merely to stand still. Old clichés such as 'cradle to grave', 'womb to tomb', have never been more relevant to personal development and occupational competence and success.

Organizations as well as their people are now beginning to become proactive in this process. Awareness is beginning to be translated into action and commitment. Large organizations have developed their own training and management development programmes, and many smaller ones have formed networks or consortiums to help meet training needs and finance delivery. The number of managers who are undertaking and completing programmes leading to qualifications such as Certificate, Diploma and Masters degree is increasing annually.

At the same time, our knowledge and understanding of the learning process in the adult has increased enormously in recent years. This is being reflected in change from the traditional methods of business education and training. Today the emphasis is moving away from the teaching to the learning, from the tutor to the learner. The emphasis in the training methods adopted and the responsibility for the learning rests very firmly with the learner. The late Winston Churchill's observation, made many years ago, that 'I love to learn but I hate being taught' has at last been acknowledged.

It is against this background of changing attitudes, knowledge and methods that in 1989 I produced the manuscript for the first edition of this book. I said then that the number of people who will be involved in training and development in the years ahead will increase as provision widens and increases, and that prediction has proved correct. The trend for increasing involvement of line managers in training and development, and the increase in the number of informal training and development opportunities in the workplace has accelerated this trend. For those suddenly thrown in at the deep end it can be a traumatic experience. I hope that the content of this book will help reduce the trauma, the period of 'trial and error' learning and will help people develop their training skills.

While the new edition is again largely targeted at the inexperienced trainer who is starting a career in training and development, it is also aimed at the more experienced trainer who may need to consider alternative ideas and approaches. This is one reason why a section on Facilitation has been added to Chapter 7 in response to the growth of action learning programmes internationally.

This section, along with other new sections have been written in response to changes in training and development which have taken place in the past six years and also in response to the feedback I have received on the first edition from readers and reviewers. These have come from around the world and have been constructive, helpful and encouraging. A very sincere thanks to everyone who contributed, and I hope the second edition will encourage similar feedback.

One of the great appeals of the first edition was, according to the feedback, its simplicity and practical application. While I have introduced some new theories and concepts, for example in Chapter 4 on 'Learning Theory', I hope the same comments still apply. There is a fine line between striving for academic credibility and achieving practical relevance and I hope I have not fallen between the two stools.

The book should also serve as a course text and as a launching pad for those undertaking serious study for a qualification in training and development. It should be a useful text for those taking a Certificate or Diploma in Training and Development (and in the UK, NVQ Levels 3– 5), while for those aspiring higher, the expanded Further Reading section at the end of each chapter will provide a starting point for those who want to study and practice in greater depth in the relevant field.

As before, I cannot complete the introduction without a few words of thanks to so many people who have shared their views and experience with me, and also helped, supported and influenced my thinking during my career. They are too numerous to mention by name, but special thanks are due to:

● the numerous adult students and managers who have attended programmes with which I have been involved in Europe, the USA, and South East Asia;

- Brian Hirst, formerly Head of Business and Management Studies at Keighley Technical College, who first stressed to me that education is for the benefit of the learner;
- Merle E. Peacock, Jnr, Superintendent of Schools, MSAD No. 11, Gardiner, Maine, USA, and the School Board, for opening the door to a once-in-a-lifetime opportunity. The experience will never be forgotten;
- Malcolm S. Knowles, who in one day in San Antonio, Texas, made me stop and think at greater length about adult learning and who started me on a continual process of self-directed inquiry;
- Dave Francis, friend and colleague, for sharing his philosophy and expertise with me on numerous management development programmes;
- Gillian Pont for 25 years of support, and for acting as a constant sounding board for ideas;
- Simon and Nicholas Pont who continue to test my ideas as well as providing a valuable source of feedback;
- Edna Pollard, for over 20 years of friendship and support, and for typing the manuscript as diligently as ever.

The responsibility for the ideas expressed rests entirely with me, and while these ideas might provoke disagreement, my sincere wish is that they provoke thought and lead to a development of training skills. By developing these, your own development as a trainer and the personal development of your learners should be greatly enhanced. Good luck in your training and development activities!

1 The training field—what it is

Training is about developing people as individuals and helping them to become more confident and competent in their lives and in their jobs. The learning process is at the core of training and the ways of, and opportunities for, learning are numerous and varied. At the end of this chapter you will be able to:

- have a wider understanding of why training is becoming more important in our society;
- identify the five stages of the training cycle, and the key components of each stage;
- identify some of the main types of training;
- list many of the roles of the trainer;
- recognize that much of training is about facilitating the learning of others.

The training field is a rapidly growing sector of our lives and has come of age as a profession. The need for training has always been present in every walk of life, but today the need is so much greater. There are many reasons for this but the most important are probably as follows.

The pace of change   The pace of change is increasingly gathering momentum. What was appropriate 10 years ago is no longer appropriate today. Indeed, in some areas of our lives what was appropriate last month is no longer appropriate today. This is very different from the experience of previous generations.

Until the turn of the century (see Figure 1.1) the time-span of social change extended over several generations. One did not expect to have to cope with any significant change over a lifetime but, if so, the change would be gradual.

Today with each successive generation we can expect several periods of change and we must cope with them at a faster rate of imposition. The pace of change is accelerating. Under these conditions the knowledge and skills gained in yesteryear will no longer be sufficient to equip a person for a lifetime. They are only appropriate for a short period of time before becoming obsolete.

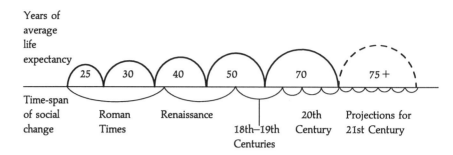

Years of
average
life
expectancy

Time-span
of social
change

| | Roman Times | Renaissance | 18th–19th Centuries | 20th Century | Projections for 21st Century |

Figure 1.1 *The relationship of the time-span of social change to individual life-span*

To illustrate the pace of change, let us consider world changes that have taken place in the period between preparing the manuscript for the first edition of this book (1989) and preparing the manuscript for its second edition (1994). During that period:

- The Berlin Wall has been demolished and many of the totalitarian leaders of Eastern Europe removed.
- The Cold War is over and Communism has collapsed throughout Eastern Europe and the former Soviet Union.
- East and West Germany have been reunited.
- The map of Eastern Europe has been redrawn.
- Britain and Argentina have restored full diplomatic relations.
- The Gulf War has taken place.
- Yugoslavia is no more.
- The Church of England has approved the ordination of women priests.
- The Single European Market has been created.
- The GATT Treaty was signed by delegates from 125 countries.
- Europe and the USA have been in the grip of the worst recession for 60 years.
- The Channel Tunnel has been completed and opened—Britain is now linked to mainland Europe.
- Israel and the PLO have signed a peace agreement.
- Apartheid has been dismantled and South Africa has held democratic elections and elected its first representative President.
- A cease-fire has been agreed in Northern Ireland and peace talks have begun.

At the micro level, a number of significant changes have gathered pace which impact directly upon organizational life and, therefore, training needs and provision. A survey of 400 HRD executives conducted by the American Society for Training and Development (1994) identified* 36 trends that will influence workplace learning and performance in the next five years. These included:

- The emergence of a global economy and its demands, which will see the development of corporate cultures and the emergence of corporate change methods to enable all individuals and organizations to react quickly to change.

- The creation of high performance work organizations.
- The move towards universal performance standards such as the ISO 9000 series.
- Technology changes, most notably the continued migration of computer power from the mainframe, to the desk top, to the briefcase and, finally to the user's hand. Also, change in the way information will be created, stored, used and shared was rated first among technological trends expected to have an effect on training and development.
- Changing roles for the training profession. The new roles include decentralization, the shift of training delivery from professional trainers to non-trainers such as managers, team leaders and technical leaders; the shift from teaching to learning and the integration of learning into work itself; and the development of learning teams and organizations.
- Increasing government support for training revealed in everything from technology transfer to tax incentives for employers to provide more training for employees. In the USA, President Clinton created in 1993 the Office of Work Based Learning within the Department of Labour.

Such enormous changes at all levels must impact upon the daily lives of individuals and organizations. We must therefore develop a training strategy backed by training systems that equip and empower individuals to cope with change. We need to move away from traditional methods of transmitting knowledge to helping people to learn how to learn. The emphasis should change from *what*, i.e., what knowledge or skill we impart, to *how*, i.e., how do we help people to learn, to ask questions and to acquire the skills of self-directed enquiry?

The attitude of employers

The attitude of employers to training is changing. Many are now beginning to see it not as a cost but as an investment. The awareness in management development, generated in the 1980s in the UK by the reports of Coopers and Lybrand, Constable and McCormick, and Handy, is at long last beginning to be translated into commitment. The implications of the quotation 'If you think training is expensive, try ignorance' are beginning to be realized and acted upon.

The attitude of individuals

The attitude of individuals to personal development is changing. We have begun to realize that training and development are lifelong processes, that the ability to learn does not necessarily decline sharply with age, that our potential could be infinitesimal and that personal development is important for both individual growth and occupational success.

Many employers are becoming aware of this shift in individual attitudes. Nowhere is this more evident than among the generation born in the 1960s, dubbed 'Generation X' in the American novel of the same name written by Douglas Coupland. This new generation frequently views personal development as more important than money, power, or even comfort at work. Professor John Hunt of the London Business School, in an extensive research project with a sample of over 20 000 managers, found that attitudes among managers had changed in the past two decades. Whereas in the 1970s power was the most important motivator, in the 1990s autonomy and independence had risen in importance, with the acquisition of new skills of great importance among 'Generation X'.

Against this backdrop of change—at the individual, organizational and societal level—is an evolution of the training provision required to meet conflicting interests. Employers and employees are wanting a full return on their investment, with the former, particularly if they are 'footing the bill', seeking added value and bottom-line results. The types of training on offer can be grouped as follows:

1 *Technical and vocational training*   Has a heavy emphasis on skills or competencies. In the UK this type of training, backed often by government funding and linked to qualification routes (GNVQ or NVQ—General and National Vocational Qualifications), has expanded rapidly in an attempt to meet skills shortages. Management training has also become more competency based, often linked into the NVQ framework. In the business school world, employers are having an increasing influence on content with the result that many qualification programmes (Certificate, Diploma, Masters degree) have a work-related project as part of the assessed programme, which will give the employer the chance to implement some of the recommendations of the project report.
2 *Personal development programmes*   The demand for these programmes has grown considerably, with courses abounding in such areas as stress management, assertiveness training, women in management, creative problem solving, team working, etc., in addition to the more standard range of management skills programmes. Individuals are also looking for added value and, in addition to valuable insights into self and personal development, are seeking to use these courses attended to build up a portfolio of evidence to obtain 'credits' towards a recognized qualification. As a result, academic institutions are becoming more flexible in their assessment procedures.

With the growth in the training market, training is now available from a variety of sources. Large organizations provide their own and some companies form consortiums to widen their provision. In addition, there are numerous public and private educational institutions, professional associations, consultancies, home study, television and other media. All these providers offer a variety of approaches which must be matched to the needs of the individual and the organization.

The goal of all these media should be to provide individual satisfaction and development so that the employing organization can also benefit. The more that people can broaden their knowledge of the training function—particularly through the variety of techniques available—the more likely will they be able to give satisfaction. That should also increase competence, confidence and result in personal growth.

The contribution of training to the business

Trainers must be aware of the close relationship between training and profit. Training for the sake of training is not the order of the day. In order for training personnel to make a case to senior management for a bigger slice of the cake, they will have to show that training achieves tangible bottom-line results. Senior decision makers must be made to view training as an investment; not only is training needed to create a skilled workforce, but also to maintain the high level of skills demanded by the constantly changing workplace and to equip people to meet future demands.

In order to add value to the business, training should accord with the direction of the corporate and business strategy—information which should cascade down the organization from senior management. Training provision should therefore help meet the business needs. This is represented diagrammatically in Fig. 1.2. Trainers must use every opportunity to give feedback on success, particularly upon the impact on the business, to senior management.

In the UK the Investors in People (IIP) award, which was launched in 1991, requires an organization to make and demonstrate a commitment from the top to develop its people in order to achieve its business

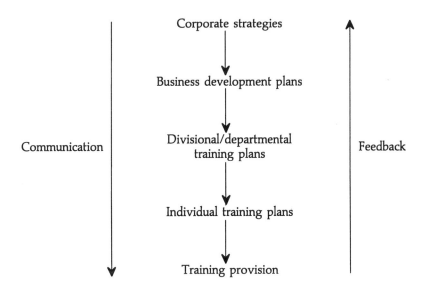

Figure 1.2 *The relationship between business needs and training provision*

objectives. In the first three years of its existence, about 11 000 organizations committed themselves to achieving the national standard. If the training provision is not delivered professionally then the quality of learning suffers, with the strong possibility that individual competence in the workplace may fall—with adverse effects upon business performance. Much of the content of this book is aimed at helping the trainer to be more professional and competent at up-front training so that the benefits to participants, and ultimately to the business, are maximized.

The training cycle

Training can be viewed as a cyclical process which is ongoing. There are five distinct phases in the cycle, all of which logically follow on from the previous stage:

1 Analysing training needs
2 Planning and designing the training approach
3 Developing the training materials
4 Delivering the training
5 Evaluating the training

The evaluation stage not only cycles back into stage 1 but also cycles back into the other three. Evaluation must be an ongoing process if training product and performance are to be refined and improved (see Figure 1.3).

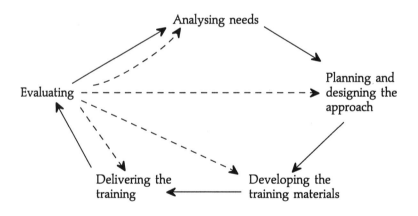

Figure 1.3   *The training cycle*

Let us look at the five stages in the cycle in a little more detail.

Analysing training needs

There are three main areas in which this analysis may take place:

1 *Needs at organizational level.* Where in the organization is training most needed?

2 *Needs at occupational level.* What is needed in terms of skill, knowledge and attitude so that the duties of various jobs can be effectively and competently carried out? This is the process of job analysis.

3 *Needs at individual level.* Who needs training in what? What is needed by individuals to bridge the competency gap between where they are now and where they should be in terms of skill, knowledge and attitude? This is the process of needs assessment.

The exact relative importance of the three areas will vary from situation to situation, but the final stage will always involve an identification of the people to be trained and the competency gap to be bridged.

Planning and designing the training approach

Like the analysis stage, a great deal of information gathering is required, particularly if you are involved with a new programme. It is also worth spending plenty of time on this phase. There is often a tendency to skate over the planning and rush into some sort of action.

The importance of planning cannot be overemphasized: 'Failing to plan is planning to fail'. The time invested in good planning will reap benefits later in the cycle.

Among the tasks that have to be addressed in this phase are:

- defining the learning objectives of the training
- deciding on the most appropriate methods of training
- deciding on the staffing and support
- selecting from the variety of media
- deciding upon content
- identifying evaluation tools
- deciding on prerequisites and pre-course preparation for the learners
- organizing and sequencing the training.

Developing the training materials

This is the stage when the work of the two previous stages is integrated into a complete set of materials to assist course delivery and meet the stated learning objectives. This is the most time-consuming part of the cycle, particularly when developing or customizing a course. It will only take up less time than the delivery stage with a course that has run many times.

Among the training materials that need to be developed and assembled are:

- course outlines
- session plans
- learner materials—workbooks, reading, handouts, etc.
- audio-visual aids—OHP transparencies, films, flip charts, etc.
- evaluation sheets.

Other important activities have to be carried out during this stage:

- background reading so that one is up-to-date on the subject
- reviewing existing materials and altering or replacing them
- briefing the tutors
- fitting individual training sessions into a logical sequence so that it all 'hangs together', which, with a new course, may require several 'trial and error' runs
- taking care of all the administrative arrangements, etc.—e.g. booking venue and such administrative details as joining instructions
- validating new materials—e.g. films, videos—before the event.

Delivering the training

This is the stage when (hopefully!) it all comes together. If the planning and preparation have been thorough, then the chances of success are vastly increased.

With the advent of participatory methods the role of the trainer has extended well beyond merely presenting. Facilitating, motivating, inspiring, leading, coordinating, managing and evaluating are just a few of the many roles that will be required.

Evaluating the training

This is an often neglected but vitally important part of the cycle. It involves some evaluation of the following:

1 Self—from self-analysis, evaluation forms and feedback from colleagues in the training team. Could you have done better? Are there areas for improvement?
2 The course materials. Do they need replacing, revising, updating?
3 The whole course—self, learners, observers
4 Segments of the course—self, learners, observers
5 Follow-up inquiry in terms of improved performance or behaviour in the work situation. How effective has been the transfer of learning to the real world? This stage only ceases when the course is no longer relevant.

These five stages help to bring about a change in the delegates' behaviour. This change is called *learning* and without it there has been no effective training.

Types of training

Two broad categories of training exist:

1 *Trainer controlled.* A good example is the lecture.
2 *Learner controlled.* A good example would be a distance learning package; another would be a mature Action Learning Set, receiving very little help or advice from the facilitator.

All learning is essentially the responsibility of the learners. The more they put into the experience, the more they tend to get out of it. This would apply to the whole range of learning opportunities that are available from the lecture (did the learners concentrate and listen?) to the participatory methods (did they prepare and risk themselves?) to everyday learning opportunities (were they aware of the situation and did they evaluate what was observed and experienced?). Very often learning is consolidated and integrated following a period of contemplation and implementation, which requires commitment.

The main types of training may be summarized as follows.

Classroom This can vary greatly in approach from the traditional method in which the trainer adopts the role of lecturer, with little or no student participation, to where the trainer adopts the role of facilitator—with the style ranging from non-directive to directive.

A classroom situation in which the emphasis is on learner participation certainly produces greater learner enjoyment and, usually, more effective learning.

Outdoors This form of training has been widely used for a number of years and has probably been most used by the armed forces, particularly in such fields as leadership training and team-building. An increasing number of companies are now using such an approach.

It has many recommendations, not least that it requires a whole-hearted commitment, individual defences are quickly lowered and barriers to learning are removed in a very non-structured environment.

Some writers might argue that it lacks the academic rigour of classroom training, but if it is linked meaningfully with classroom input and debriefing, a great deal of effective learning and development can take place.

Computer-assisted learning This is largely a refinement of programmed learning in which individuals work through written material in a programmed way. Learners progress in a step-by-step fashion, having received feedback on their responses.

Such programmed learning has become more sophisticated in recent years with the advent of computers, videos and video discs. Individuals can work at home if they have their own PC or on a work station at work, which may form part of an open learning facility.

One of the great advantages of such training is flexibility—the learners can progress at their own pace and wherever they want. The disadvantages are isolation, which can result in low motivation and reduced commitment, and cost. With some of the interactive video packages on the market the cost of the hardware and software can be several thousand pounds. A detailed cost-benefit analysis is required before an investment of such magnitude is undertaken.

Simulation This type of training is very participative and is used mainly for skills training. It may reinforce other types of training, e.g. classroom training.

As far as possible simulation training is linked to the 'real world'. Good examples are 'in-tray' exercises, which are used to train managers in decision-making, or as part of an assessment centre—a method increasingly used in managerial selection.

Another good example is flight simulation, which is a realistic imitation of the real world. This trains pilots in flying skills and also teaches them to deal with emergencies on the aircraft.

Training methods

Within the types of training, some flexibility exists as to the *methods* used. These are discussed in detail later in the book. Equally, within the methods, a variety of media can be used—overhead projectors, flip charts, films, slides, etc.—which can enhance the method of delivery. These are also discussed later in the book.

As a general rule try to aim for variety in both method and media—it breaks up the learner's day and allows the message to get through on more than one channel.

The role of the trainer

The obvious role of the trainer is as a *deliverer*, so the key competency to acquire is *presenting*. A trainer should be good at presenting information so that the attention of the audience is held and the information is accurately conveyed.

Training, however, is much, much more and in many situations the presenting role is one of the least important. Merely considering the five stages in the training cycle indicates that numerous roles are demanded: the skills of needs analysis are very different from presenting, the skills of designing a course are very different from evaluation, the skills of writing resource material are very different from group management, and so on. And many more roles have to be performed, both in the group situation and outside of it. A quick brainstorming of some of the roles required might be as follows:

presenter   psychologist   subject expert   mentor   'agony aunt' learner   coach   person   listener   counsellor   planner   leader evaluator   creator   manager   writer   innovator   administrator organizer   motivator   diffuser   persuader   seller   role model technician   catalyst   'dogsbody'   and many more.

This is an awesome list and none of us can be excellent at all of them. It is more a question of being aware of our strengths, playing to them and finding ways to combat the weaknesses. We can concentrate on developing the weaknesses or we can ensure that other people are involved, either from the training team, from members of the group or by requesting external assistance, such as a technician. The important thing is that the event goes well and the learners learn and leave as satisfied customers.

Thus the main role of the trainer is that of a *facilitator*—you facilitate by the best method available, using the resources available, the learning and development of the group. While most of this role will be undertaken when the group is actually together, much of it also takes place elsewhere, e.g. at the needs analysis stage where one often facilitates the identification of training needs and the release of individuals for training.

Within the training situation most of the roles of the facilitator fall into three distinct categories, and these are worthy of further elaboration.

Subject expert

Our delegates expect you to know something about the subject and the more you know and communicate that knowledge, the more your credibility increases. Thus it is an important part of your own development to update your knowledge of the field.

Our delegates do not expect you to know everything. Nobody can be a complete fountain of knowledge and if you don't know, admit it—don't flannel. A useful tip here is to recognize any expertise within the group and use it when appropriate. Also, with a very specialized field, consider bringing in an expert for a 'one-off'. Not only does it give expert input of knowledge, it also exposes delegates to a change of style which is often beneficial. One cautionary note—do not create such an aura of expertise that you become unapproachable. Credible experts with the human touch are far more respected. For most people, merely being natural is the best way to achieve this.

Method expert

As will be discussed later in the book, there are numerous learning methods available and you should be familiar with most and feel comfortable and competent with a few.

Part of your role is to exercise sound, professional judgement as to the best method of helping your delegates learn, and sometimes during the event your role can be very low key.

Becoming competent with a variety of learning methods should be a constant goal and should be part of your own professional development. Watch other trainers and learn from them, and risk yourself on occasions and experiment. As in all walks of life, it is only when we risk ourselves that true growth and development occur.

Group manager

This is the area in which the facilitation skills are most obvious. Trainers require a high level of interpersonal skills to be able to manage (not control) a group. The style and role can change from motivator to leader to counsellor, according to the situation.

Trainers must be sensitive to group atmosphere and mood as well as to the individuals present. They need to be able to analyse individuals as well as the group. They need to have some understanding of individual and group psychology, although they do not need to become experts.

Of the three main areas, this is the one where the skills take longest to acquire. Subject competency can be acquired fairly quickly—group facilitation skills take much longer. A good and experienced group facilitator has a skill of enormous power and is able to really harness the synergy within the group to achieve powerful and lasting learning. It is a competency you should strive to acquire and is best acquired through practice.

The foregoing is a general list to give a broad picture. More detail on many of the roles and how to perform them more competently is included in later chapters.

Exercises

1 Consider a trainer you have observed or worked with.

   (a) What were his/her strengths?
   (b) What were his/her weaknesses?
   (c) Why was the trainer successful?
   (d) Why was the trainer unsuccessful?
   (e) What did he/she do well?
   (f) What did he/she do badly?
   (g) What did you learn from the trainer?
   (h) If there was a training team, how did the trainers complement each other?

2 Consider three training situations in which you have been involved.

   (a) For each one consider the roles played by the trainer(s).
   (b) How did the trainer(s) help learning?
   (c) What could have been done better to improve learning?

3 Consider any involvement you have had in the following.

   (a) Classroom training.
   (b) Outdoor education.
   (c) Training involving sophisticated hardware and software.
   (d) Simulations.

   How effective were each in achieving their objectives? Why?

4 Think of three different trainers you have seen who had different styles. What were those styles? How effective were they?

5 A list of major world changes that have happened in the period 1989–94 was given earlier in the chapter. List some of the changes that have taken place in your life in the past five years. What do you need to do to address these changes?

Summary

The following are the main points with regard to training:

- Training is becoming more widely accepted and recognized as a way of helping individuals and organizations cope with change and develop.
- Training is a cyclical process with five main stages: analysing, planning and designing, developing, delivering, evaluating.
- There are many types of training available and learner participation achieves best results.
- Training is not just presenting; it requires a successful execution of a number of roles, both in and out of the classroom.
- The most important role is that of FACILITATOR of the learning process. Subject competencies, competence with learning methods and group management skills are essential for success.

Further reading

American Society for Training and Development, *The Past, Present and Future of Workplace Learning*. American Society for Training and Development, Alexandria, Virginia, 1994.

J. Bank, *Outdoor Development for Managers* (2nd edn). Gower, Aldershot, 1994.

R. Bennett (ed.), 'The right role', in *Improving Trainer Effectiveness*. Gower, Aldershot, 1988.

T. Bentley, *The Business of Training: Achieving Success in Changing World Markets*. McGraw-Hill, Maidenhead, 1991.

R. Buckley and Jim Caple, *The Theory and Practice of Training* (2nd edn). Kogan Page, London, 1992.

J. Constable and R. McCormick, *The Making of British Managers*. BIM and CBI, London, 1987.

Coopers and Lybrand Associates, *Challenge to Complacency*. MSC, Sheffield, November 1985.

D. Coupland, *Generation X*. Abacus, London, 1994.

C. Handy *et al.*, *The Making of Managers: A Report on Management Education, Training and Development in USA, West Germany, France, Japan and the UK*. NEDO, MSC and BIM, London, 1987.

K. Jones, *A Handbook for Teachers and Trainers*. Kogan Page, London, 1982.

L. Nadler, 'The variety of training roles', *Industrial and Commercial Training*, 1969, Vol. 1, No. 1.

R. Petersen, *Training Needs Analysis in the Workplace*. Kogan Page, London, 1992.

J. W. Pfeiffer and J. G. Jones (eds), *The Annual Handbook for Group Facilitators* (19 vols). University Associates, San Diego, California, 1972–96.

P. R. Pinto and J. W. Walker, *A Study of Training Development Roles and Competencies*. American Society for Training and Development, Washington, D.C., 1978.

T. Pont, *Investing in Training and Development: Turning Interest into Capital*. Kogan Page, London, 1995.

L. Rae, *The Skills of Training. A Guide for Managers and Practitioners* (2nd edn). Gower, Aldershot, 1991.

D. Reay, *Identifying Training Needs*. Kogan Page, London, 1994.

M. A. Reid, H. Barrington and J. Kenney, *Training Interventions: managing employee development* (3rd edn). Institute of Personnel Management, London, 1992.

2 Designing the course

The designing of a course from nothing can appear a daunting and awesome task, not to mention the time involved. If one adopts a systematic approach then it can greatly help clarify thinking and create a framework for development.

At the end of this chapter, you will be able to:

- identify the main stages in the systematic approach to course design;
- identify some of the main considerations for each of the nine stages in the systematic approach;
- use the systematic approach as a framework for the design of future courses.

Many of us have been contacted by someone and asked to take a course. It may vary from a short-duration adult education class at the local centre to a full workshop or programme for senior managers in a famous and exotic international location.

Whatever the location or whatever the level, the role of the trainer is to design a meaningful learning experience for the participants, starting from a blank sheet of paper. At this stage the delivery of the programme seems a million miles away and a multitude of questions begin to emerge, all of which need answering before any design and delivery can begin to take place. Below is a list of the kind of questions that are soon asked and need answering.

Who are the delegates?
How many delegates
What is their educational level?
What is their seniority?
Why are they coming?
What do they hope to get out of the programme?
Where is it to be held?
What are the facilities?
What visual aids, etc., are available?
What body of knowledge *must* I cover?
should I cover?
could I cover?

What *skills* are they hoping to acquire?
To what level of competency?
Why is the organization sending them?
What are the objectives of the programme? Individual objectives?
　　Organizational objectives?
What are the times of the course?
What is the duration of the course?
What methods should I employ?
Which resource material will I need to deliver the programme?
Will I be on my own?
Will others be helping me?
How will I know if the course has met its objectives?

These are just a sample of the kinds of question that come into the mind of the trainer in quickfire succession. In order to give clarity of thinking and purpose to this 'mish-mash' of thoughts, it helps to approach the situation in a systematic manner.

The main ideas behind the systematic approach are:

1 that as a trainer you should have responsibility for planning the system in which the self-directing needs of your students can be satisfied so that they can learn;
2 that you have fully analysed and understood the skill and knowledge that your students must develop and the level of competence they should acquire;
3 that from this analysis you will be able to construct a list of objectives to help you design the course and give you some indication as to the resources you will need;
4 once you have clarified your objectives, then you can devise an appropriate range of learning materials to meet those objectives;
5 that if you fail to meet your objectives, then you must ask *why* and take the appropriate action to bridge the learning or competency gap.

The nine stages of the systematic approach

Put into a systematic or sequential series of nine stages, these would be the questions you would ask and answer:

1 What is the general aim of the course?
2 What are the key learning objectives?
3 What should be included in the course in terms of knowledge, skills and attitude modification?
4 What are the most appropriate methods of learning to help achieve the objectives?
5 What resources are needed to use these methods?
6 How can the course best be designed to meet the above criteria?
7 What is the best way of presenting/delivering the course?
8 How can the success of the programme be evaluated?
9 How can the programme be refined or improved?

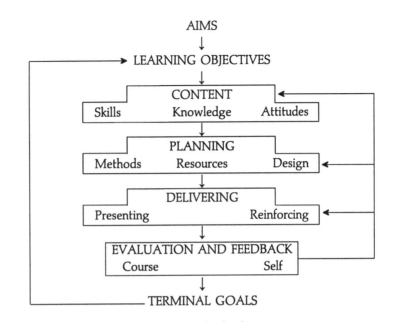

Figure 2.1   *The systematic approach to the development of a course*

The sequence is shown diagrammatically in Figure 2.1.

1 Defining the aims   One is often asked, 'What is the difference between an aim and an objective?' In general, an aim represents the long-term goals of the course. What do we hope to achieve in broad terms at the end? What goals must the students attain by the end of the programme? Once the overall aims are determined the trainer can then begin to consider the detailed objectives for the course.

2 Defining learning objectives   Learning objectives have also been called performance objectives and behavioural objectives. Whatever the terminology, objectives must be clearly defined.

An objective is a precise goal stated in measurable quantitative or qualitative terms. It is of little use to you in designing a course if vague, woolly terminology is used in defining the objectives.

There are three simple rules to help you define and write down your objectives to enable you to plan your course:

1 What can you reasonably expect your students to be able to do, know or think by the end of the course? If you start from the end product or final performance that is expected, it is much easier to plan the first steps.
2 Analyse this final performance into the three basic types of learning—knowledge, skills and attitude change. The relative importance of the three types will vary, but they are usually present in differing degrees. All courses have a knowledge (cognitive)

content. All teachers are in the business of attitude change (affective learning)—whether it be merely changing the students' attitudes to a learning process—and the amount of skill acquisition will vary according to the course.

3 Be specific in the words you use. It will help you if you avoid vague words such as 'knowledge', 'show', 'understand', 'appreciate' and use words such as 'list', 'identify', 'use', 'state', 'compare', 'define'.

3 Determining the content

Once the objectives have been decided, it is helpful to draft a course outline of the content needed to provide the delegates with the skills, knowledge and attitudes identified in the objectives. These topics should be arranged in a teaching/learning sequence.

The next stage is to use the objectives and content outline to develop a course of study. The course of study should:

- meet the specific and general objectives of the course;
- cover the main topics with supporting detail arranged in a teaching/learning sequence;
- contain suggestions as to the most effective and efficient ways of presenting the material;
- suggest ways in which your delegates' learning can be reinforced by practical experience;
- state or consider the range of teaching aids or media needed to present or assist the presentation of material;
- consider ways of evaluating the progress of the individual or group against objectives.

It is always helpful to discuss your thoughts or ideas with others, especially those with more experience. This should help you check that you have made no glaring omissions and can help you crystallize your own thoughts and ideas.

4 Choosing your method

It would be nice and easy to have a grid of all the teaching methods linked to the learning objective so that it would merely be a case of 'reading off' what the appropriate method should be.

Unfortunately it is not usually as easy as this. There are numerous methods of teaching available and while it is true that some methods are best suited to certain learning objectives there is usually some element of choice.

There are, of course, other variables which impact upon the choice of method.

Your students' preferences, abilities and personalities

Recent research, particularly in the area of learning styles, indicates that we all have developed preferred learning habits or styles that help us benefit more from some experiences than from others.

At this point it is not the intention to describe the four styles in detail, it will suffice to say that different personality types with differing levels of intelligence will respond differently to, and perhaps get less/more out of, certain situations than others (see Chapter 5).

Your own preferences and abilities

The skills of facilitating a learning experience for adults are skills that are acquired over a long period of time. This applies even more when the group members are highly intelligent, motivated and occupy senior positions.

Different methods require different skills. While it would be desirable to be completely at ease with all the great variety of methods, very few attain that overall level of competence. Furthermore, there is little doubt that we all have preferences for working in a certain way. Some love to give a formal lecture and inspire the audience or group with their rhetoric; others prefer to work from within the group in a quiet, self-effacing way.

The best advice that can be offered is:

1 Given that the learning objectives and the needs of the student are met, choose the method with which you feel most comfortable. That is neither being selfish nor neglecting the needs of your students; rather it is allowing you to give of your best for their benefit and groups usually respond accordingly.
2 Bring in someone else who is more competent than you in a certain method. This can be one of the great benefits of team-teaching where two or more facilitators on a programme can compensate for each other's strengths and weaknesses.

Resources available

This would include the accommodation available, audio-visual aids and the amount of help you have. You cannot do small group work if you are alone with 20 participants!

Whatever the influences or considerations, it must be said with regard to method that one should always strive for *variety*. It exploits the sense of curiosity, enjoyment, excitement, interest and arousal in both trainer and participant alike. In a nutshell, it prevents staleness setting in.

Variety of method is also an important way of catering for the heterogeneity that exists in groups. Even if the educational attainment level is similar, we know that a variety of preferred styles of learning exist. By varying the method we can cater for all preferences within the group and at the same time give everyone the chance to develop other styles of learning, in much the same way that we would exercise and develop a muscle.

5 Determining the resources

In an ideal world a trainer will not be bound by a shortage of resources. It would merely be a case of deciding upon the ideal programme and obtaining the necessary resources. Unfortunately, this is rarely the case and the trainer has to consider the resources that are available and tailor the course accordingly. It can happen that, having decided upon the ideal method, the resources are not available. It is therefore advisable to enquire about and consider availability of resources before designing the course.

Resources can be divided into two main categories:

1 *Physical resources*

- location of course
- size of room and seating
- audio-visual aids
- course materials—handouts, case studies, etc.

2 *Human resources*

- self
- colleague(s)
- course members.

Never underestimate the influence of the course members as a resource. They bring a wealth of experience and can help facilitate the learning of their peers.

6 Designing the course

To date we have identified aims, objectives, content, methods and resources. Now comes the final part of the preparation when we actually put it all together and design the course, section by section. This involves deciding on a plan of action, i.e. a lesson or session plan. This provides you with the orderly procedures for conducting or facilitating a session efficiently. It should not be long (two pages at the most) but should be complete and practical. It should be written or sectioned in a format that is helpful and meaningful to you, the trainer, and it should give you confidence—not only is it proof that you have prepared adequately, but it is your 'prop' if you need it.

The main points of a session plan include:

- topic
- objectives—the key part
- time required and timings
- learning methods
- audio-visual aids required
- questions for checking and review
- assignment(s) and references.

The importance of planning cannot be overemphasized, however experienced you are. Part of the planning process is mental and part is written. Generally, the more inexperienced we are, the more we tend to feel the need to develop written session plans, which give us confidence and serve as a guide to move the learning along in an orderly fashion.

A series of session plans will constitute your course and are useful because they:

- plan for a smooth transition from previous sessions to new material
- ensure sequential and adequate presentation of material
- offer time controls
- provide for proper use of methods, aids and equipment
- establish a record of material presented and training accomplished
- serve as a guide to the trainer so that important points are not omitted
- help to avoid attempted detours by students and keep you on schedule (if appropriate).

The session plan is your guide and script. It should be flexible to accommodate interruptions, questions and the lack of understanding on the part of the learners. Departures from the written plan can be expected as the learners fail to understand some aspect of the work, become interested in a particular part of the session, or contribute to the session from their own experiences. Sometimes a teaching plan may be used over and over again with the occasional minor revision to adjust to changing needs and situations.

There are numerous types of standardized lesson or session plans that can be used. Many trainers have adopted one to suit their own situations.

Below is one session plan form that can be modified according to your own situation.

Topic:
Time and length:
Learning objective(s):
Group/Class/Target audience:
Student preparation:
Teaching aids required:
Materials for student use:
Handouts required:
Evaluation:
Lesson outline:
    Timing
    Key points
    Delivery sequence
    Briefing for following assignment

Comments and review to improve

The key to any session plan is the listing of objectives. Always keep these in your mind and consider the behaviour that your learners will be capable of at the end of the session which they were not capable of at the start. This will not only help you focus more clearly, but also help you recognize when the desired changes or results have been accomplished. If you are unsure of what to expect as a result of your session, you are less likely to know if it happened.

No session plan is perfect and so always consider ways to improve it. Always review it—and do so soon after the event while it is still fresh in your mind. The session plan is your tool to help you—beforehand to prepare, during the lesson to help conduct a successful learning experience, and afterwards to evaluate whether you achieved your objectives.

7 Presenting the course If you have thoroughly prepared, your chances of success are high. Much will be said later in the book about the conducting of the first session, the use of visual aids, techniques of presentation, learning methods, etc., so it will suffice here to give only a broad outline.

Always begin by 'tuning-in' to the group and 'where they are at', i.e. what are their needs and what do they already know? Relating the start to their position begins to increase feelings of security and will get initial commitment.

In presenting new information, show how it builds on the existing body of knowledge. The teaching methods you select depend on your personal choice and preferences, the material being presented and the level of students in the group. By choosing an appropriate method, you quickly obtain individual interest and attention so that group management is made easier. From experience you quickly learn the kind of presentation that is best suited to different situations. This develops your self-confidence, improves your feelings of security and rapport with the group, and shows that your training is producing real learning.

In presenting each session, always err on the side of simplicity. Look for individual interest and expertise and use it wherever appropriate. Aim for variety during the presentation and use flip charts, overhead projectors, films, filmstrips, etc., if they enhance your message. Allow time for questions and checking that the key points of your presentation have been assimilated. Allow opportunities later in the course for reinforcement of the learning.

Afterwards it may help you to note down the good aspects and areas for improvement in your session. What have *you* learned, and how can your presentation be improved? This is particularly important if you will have to repeat the session at some future date. If you must, rewrite your presentation or session plan.

In the presentation stage you should give the information in orderly steps, working from the simple to the more complex and arranging the presentation in the best possible learning sequence. Remember also, never make your session too long—the quality of learning is not directly related to the length of your session. Once the information has been presented, your learners should have the opportunity to use it, apply it, and work with it as soon as possible. This begins the reinforcement process, introduces variety and may offer the opportunity to correct misunderstandings, offer additional information and provide individual instruction.

The learning process is now focused on the learner. Your role becomes much more of a facilitator, but you should be readily available to offer help or support. Learners usually enjoy this practical or participative style—they can relate it to themselves and their situation; they can test and apply new concepts or skills; and they can achieve success, which is a great motivator, and so they are ready to learn more.

The practical session needs to be carefully planned to ensure that the task, materials and equipment are available and working for all the participants to use. If it is poorly planned then your own credibility could suffer greatly.

8 Evaluating the course
This step helps to determine the effectiveness of the learning. It is much easier to evaluate knowledge and skills than attitude change. For the knowledge component, written or oral questions may be used. They should test the key points and highlight any individual development points. For the skills component, a performance test may be used—learners carry out a task and they are observed and rated.

During the planning stage you will have been aware of items that were included unnecessarily or of relevant items that were omitted. During the evaluation stage you will become more acutely aware of the need for revision, having piloted the course. Most courses, from inception, need a few deliveries before becoming acceptable and even then new ideas, methods, etc., should be incorporated wherever appropriate.

The main objective of any learning evaluation is for the individuals to realize their progress and their own developmental needs. If they are allowed to realize that themselves, rather than being told, then there is greater acceptance and greater commitment to continue learning and to develop. Ownership of their own action plan and commitment to it must surely be the objective of all training courses.

9 Review to improve
This is the final stage of the evaluation in which we focus on ourselves and look to the future. It involves considering:

- how successful we were in enabling our learners to achieve their objectives;
- how successful we were as trainers in presenting, in our choice of methods, visual aids, etc.

In short, how can we improve the course and our performance so that we can do a more professional job? We must learn from analysing our successes and failures and identifying their causes. Feedback here is vital and we must seek it from our learners and from our colleagues. At times such feedback may be painful, but if we are to learn and develop then we must seek honest feedback and seek to improve. After all, 'sauce for our learners must be sauce for ourselves'.

An example of course design

The marketing director of a pharmaceutical company is concerned about the high level of staff turnover among medical representatives and the problem of poor performance among some representatives.

The indications are that:

- the level of selection interviewing skills among regional managers is poor
- the regional managers' knowledge of company disciplinary procedure is minimal.

You are asked to design and deliver a two-day course for eight people to improve their regional managers' knowledge of interviewing. This is the **aim** of the course.

Objectives (remember to look at the final performance)   As a result of attending this course, delegates will be able to:

- list objectives for interviews
- draw up a person specification for a post
- plan and conduct an effective interview for
  - selection purposes
  - disciplinary purposes
- know and be able to use the 7-point plan at a selection interview
- use good questioning technique
- use good listening technique
- explain the company disciplinary procedure
- document and assess the evidence and make a recommendation.

Planning   Possible methods to use:

1 Lectures
2 Discussions
3 Case studies
4 Role plays
5 Observation and imitation
6 Films
7 Projects

Possible resources required:

1 Overhead projector (OHP) and transparencies
2 Flip charts, etc.
3 Case study material—best to relate to real-life situations so it 'comes alive' for the participants
4 Closed-circuit television (CCTV)
5 Films or videos
6 16 mm projector or video recorder
7 Handouts
8 Accommodation.

Based upon the foregoing, the design of the two days in broad outline could be as follows.

			Method
Day 1	9.00	Introductions	
		Expectations	
		Objectives	
		Content and method	
		— selection interviewing	
		— discipline	
		— use of practical exercises	
		(role plays using CCTV)	
	9.45	Interviewing—general principles	Lecture
	10.15	Coffee	
	10.30	Selection interviewing	
		1 The application form and employee	
		specification	Lecture
		2 Analysing the CV—exercise	Project
		3 The 7-point plan	Lecture
		4 Questioning technique and exercises	Lecture and project
		5 Listening and exercises	Lecture and project
		6 Film	
		7 Discussion	Discussion
		8 Review	
	12.45	Lunch	
	1.45	Practice interviews—using CVs of	
		previous applicants	
		4 × 1 hour interviews	
		— case study and role play	
		— critique and debrief using peer	
		observation and CCTV	
		NB Each case study is different	
	5.45	Plenary session—share and compare	
		Learning review	
		Reading assignment	
	6.00	Disperse	
Day 2	9.00	Issues arising from Day 1	
		Discussion	Discussion
	9.15	The company disciplinary procedure	Lecture
		Discussion	Discussion
	9.45	The disciplinary interview—stages	Lecture
		Discussion	Discussion
		Film	Film
		Discussion	Discussion
	10.30	Coffee	
	10.45	Practice interviews	
		2 × 1 hour interviews	
		— case study and role play	Case study & role play

− critique and debrief using peer observation and CCTV	*Method*
− discussion	*Discussion*

1.15   Lunch
2.15   Practical disciplinary interviews
        2 × 1 hour interviews

− case study and role play	*Case study* *& role play*
− critique and debrief using peer observation and CCTV	
− discussion	*Discussion*

      NB   Each case study is different. Tea
      between interviews—approx. 3.25 pm
4.20   Plenary session—share and compare
      Learning review
      Disperse

An example of a draft session plan from this course might have the following appearance:

Course: Interviewing skills for regional managers
Session: Selection interviewing
Time: 10.30 am–12.45 pm

Session outline or element	*Method content, handouts* *visual-aids, etc.*

1 The company job application form and
    specimen employee specification for
    medical rep. (10.30 am)
	• Lecture/discussion
	• 8 application forms
	• 8 job specifications
	
	                  (10 mins)

2 Analysing the CV—stress the
    importance of pre-preparation
    (10.40 am)
	• 8 specimen CVs
	• split into two syndicates,
	   examine CV and compile
	   a list of points to raise
	   at interview
	
	                  (30 mins)

3 The 7-point plan (11.10 am)	• 8 specimen company
	   assessment forms
	• brief input to describe
	   plan

Session outline or element	*Method content, handouts visual-aids, etc.*
	• any questions • handout (20 mins)
4 Questioning technique (11.30 am)	• types of questions—input • exercise to spot errors in questioning—8 handouts • in pairs do exercise • share in plenary handout (25 mins)
5 Listening (11.55 am)	• input about techniques of summarizing • in pairs, exercise to practise it • input on technique of reflecting • in pairs, exercise to practise it • discussion • give out handouts (25 mins)
6 Film (12.20 pm)	• show 'Man Hunt' • discussion • relate to earlier parts of a session (35 mins)
7 Review of morning (12.55 pm)	• discussion (5 mins)

The level of detail required is a matter for individual choice. Inexperienced trainers will probably need to go into greater detail than experienced trainers. The important part to stress is that your preparation should enable you to do a good job and, therefore, you should plan the session to a level of detail that satisfies your comfort level and boosts your confidence.

Exercises
1 Consider a course you have been involved in designing.

    (a) How did you go about it?
    (b) What went well? Why?
    (c) What went badly? Why?
    (d) What would you repeat next time?
    (e) What would you do differently?

2 If you have to design a new course in the near future, you might like to use the nine stages in the systematic approach as a guide. Once you become familiar with it, and with using it, you will find it a useful tool in all future design work. Remember, practice makes perfect.

Summary

In order to deliver a course successfully, the main requirements are:

- determine and understand the broad aim
- establish objectives (stated in terms of future learner accomplishments)
- plan thoroughly beforehand
  - determine the content
  - choose your method(s) and strive for variety
  - be aware of available resources and assemble them
  - develop individual session plans
- competence in delivering the training
  - put delegates at ease and always relate to their needs
  - present slowly and clearly
  - check for understanding
  - involve the participants
- allow ample opportunities for reinforcement
- evaluate thoroughly
  - participants' learning
  - self.

Further reading

I. K. Davies, *Instructional Technique*. McGraw-Hill, New York, 1981.

R. Mager, *Preparing Instructional Objectives* (2nd edn). Kogan Page, London, 1991.

C. Nicolay and J. Barrette, *Assembling Course Materials: A Trainer's Action Guide*. Kogan Page, London, 1992.

G. Pask and B. Lewis, *Teaching Strategies: A Systems Approach*. Open University Press, Milton Keynes, 1972.

L. Willis and J. Daisley, *Developing Women Through Training: A Practical Handbook*. McGraw-Hill, Maidenhead, 1992.

3 Delivering the course—the start-up

The early part of any course is the most crucial. The design and content of a course may be first class, but that is no guarantee that all will go well. Much can be done behind the scenes to increase your chances of success.

At the end of this chapter you will be able to:

- identify many of the key tasks that have to be performed beforehand in preparation for the course;
- identify some of the main forms of room layout;
- list some of the things that you can do to prepare yourself;
- identify and use a method of getting the first session underway.

The course has been designed and all the preparation associated with it has been completed. You are ready to deliver. Much thought needs to be given before the first session to ensure success and it is always advisable to give yourself the best possible chances of success. While you may have a good command of the subject content and are familiar with the teaching methodology, that alone is no guarantee of success. The first session is the most crucial of the whole course. It is the time of 'weighing up', when the first impressions are made that are so vitally important. In any interactive situation it is so much easier at a later stage if you set off on the right track—it is easier to stay on track than get back on it. It is, therefore, vital that you give more attention and thought to the start-up than to any other part of the course.

The first session usually sets the tone for the rest of the course. What can we do to improve our chances of (a) making a good first impression and (b) being successful?

Preparation for the course

Before start-up

For the inexperienced trainer the time spent on this phase is much greater than for the experienced trainer. As a general rule of thumb the inexperienced trainer probably needs to spend at least three hours' preparation for every hour's presentation. Although the ratio of preparation time to presentation time may drop for the experienced trainer, it still should be carried out. Complacency is a bigger threat than inexperience and delegates are less tolerant of this than inexperience.

If advice can be given on preparation, err on the side of over-preparation rather than under-preparation. The belief that 'it will be all right on the night' tends only to hold true if you have done your homework.

To help you ensure that all the details have been taken care of, it is useful to prepare a 'trainer checklist'. Not only will this help you to ensure that everything has been carried out first time round, but it will make life easier on subsequent occasions and, perhaps, for your successor. It is also something that can be altered in the light of experience. A simple checklist is outlined below.

Course/lesson
Date
Location
Number of delegates
Number of rooms
Trainer(s)

Item/Task	Required	Done	Comments
Joining instructions (a) map (b) delegate list (c) course outline (d) transport arrangements			
Meals (a) times (b) menus (c) coffee breaks			
Recreation (a) times (b) facilities			
Accommodation reservations (a) delegates (b) trainer(s) (c) guest speaker(s)			

Item/Task	Required	Done	Comments
Training materials (a) handouts (b) exercise materials (c) films, videos, etc.			

Visual aids
(a) screen
(b) film projector(s)
(c) OHP (and spare bulb)
(d) demonstration or practice
   equipment
(e) Flip charts
   (i)   pads
   (ii) easel
   (iii) pens
   (iv) Blu-Tack or masking
      tape
   (v)   other AV devices
   (vi) extension cables			

Training room (a) layout (b) refreshments			

Materials for delegates
(a) advance materials
   e.g. reading
(b) name tags
(c) pencils
(d) paper
(e) books
(f) hole punch
(g) folders
(h) clipboards
(i) course certificate
(j) course mementos, e.g.
   photos, gifts, etc.			

Trainer materials (a) handouts (b) lesson plan (c) visuals (d) mastercopies (e) (own materials)			
Course evaluation forms			
Others			

Preparing the physical learning environment

Much of the training will take place in purpose-built accommodation, but some will also take place in rooms that were never designed with training in mind. Whatever the situation, a lot can be done to ensure that the physical environment assists rather than impedes learning—and the trainer can do much to affect the physical environment.

Wherever possible I would always advocate a visit to the learning environment *before* a course. This is even more important if the venue is unfamiliar to you as you may have the opportunity to change a poor location, either within the building or elsewhere. Even if you are using a very familiar setting and those who normally pre-prepare the room are reliable, you must still check beforehand that everything is to your satisfaction. The ultimate responsibility for ensuring that everything is satisfactory rests with the trainer.

Some of the things you can check with regard to training rooms are as follows:

1 Visit the room beforehand and assess suitability for the event.
2 Check that the size is right—not too small or too large. Does it have adjoining syndicate rooms that are appropriate?
3 Ensure that the room is designed and furnished appropriately. For example, I recently made a visit to a new hotel to inspect a training room only to discover a simulated marble floor without carpets which gave a cold and austere atmosphere.
4 Ensure there is adequate ventilation, light and heating.
5 Ensure there are adequate toilet and washing facilities.
6 Check that the environment 'feels good' and has an atmosphere conducive to interaction and learning.

Room layout

Much can be done with the furniture of a room to achieve the objectives of the course. The layout should maximize learner comfort and serve a purpose. If the learners are using equipment such as PCs then they will need a table and chair and room to lay out their worksheets, texts, instructions, etc. If, on the other hand, the group is involved in little notetaking and a variety of experiential activities, tables and chairs may get in the way and so a circle of chairs may be a much more effective arrangement. (Figures 3.1–3.8 show examples of seating plans.)

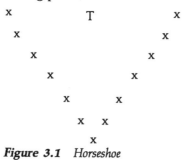

Suitable for small numbers, up to 20 learners

- Good for experiential activities.
- Promotes discussion, interaction and sense of identity.
- Informal and allows tutor to be very close to the group.
- Facilitates use of visual aids.

Figure 3.1 *Horseshoe*

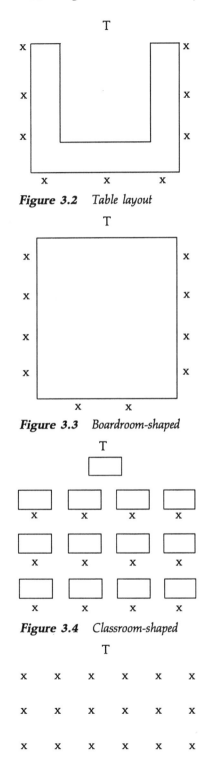

Figure 3.2 *Table layout*

Ideal for groups of less than 20.

- Gives learners plenty of space.
- Allows tutor to move freely within the group.
- Facilitates use of visual aids.
- Promotes discussion.
- Allows delegates to do much individual work.

Figure 3.3 *Boardroom-shaped*

This offers similar advantages to the previous layout, but does not allow the tutor to move as freely within the group.

Figure 3.4 *Classroom-shaped*

This is one way of accommodating large numbers.

- Involves feelings of 'back at school'.
- Does not encourage interaction and participation.

Figure 3.5 *Theatre-shaped*

This arrangement is good for formal presentations, especially to large audiences.

- Visual aids easy to use.
- Does not encourage interaction and participation.
- Sets speaker apart, which may threaten speaker who may then give below par performance.

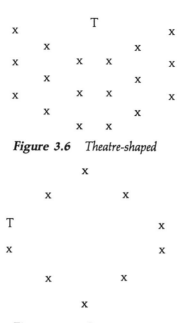

Figure 3.6 *Theatre-shaped*

The benefits and disadvantages of this arrangement are similar to those of Figure 3.5.

x

x   x

T   x

x   x

x   x

x

Figure 3.7 *Group*

Suitable for small numbers, probably up to 12.

- Intimate as it makes the tutor part of the group.
- Informal and an excellent way to promote discussion.
- Can be difficult to use OHP and other visual aids.

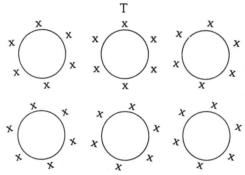

Figure 3.8 *Working conference*

Suitable for large numbers.
- Allows group work to take place during conference and after presentation.
- Groups can become inattentive and talk during presentation.
- Those with backs to speaker must turn round for speaker's presentation.

Trainer's layout   You must give yourself a place with plenty of space in which to do the tutoring or facilitating. Figure 3.9 is a diagram of how a room should be arranged for about 12 people.

Notice how much room the tutor needs for the OHP, flip chart(s), spare pens/bulbs and handouts. Give a lot of thought beforehand to how you like to work and what makes you feel comfortable. Do you like to stand or sit? Do you prefer/need to have a small table at the front? Can the delegates clearly see what you are presenting? Is your equipment correctly positioned?

Such an arrangement takes a great deal of time and should be done long before the course starts. You must never assume that the room will be ideally suited to your needs. It is the trainer's responsibility to have the

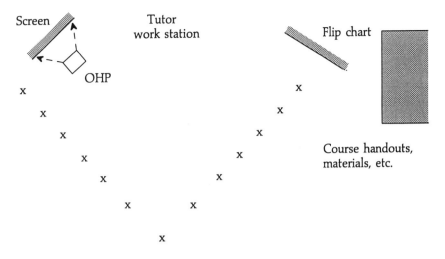

Figure 3.9 *A suggested layout of a training room*

training room furniture appropriately arranged, the course materials in order, the projectors working and focused and an adequate supply of flip chart paper and pens.

Always allow plenty of time to set out the room as you want it before the delegates arrive.

Other considerations

Trainer's tool kit box   This usually consists of two main items:

1   Your own 'masters' or folder of resource material. These are for use when you decide to digress from the printed programme or when the material you expected to be present has not materialized! In either case, with the assistance of the photocopying facility at the hotel or conference centre you can manage the situation.

2   A basic box or bag of items or things you may need at short notice, such as:

pack of file paper
Sellotape
Blu-Tack
stapler
rubber bands
correction fluid
plain file cards
OHP extending pointer
paper clips
hole punch, 2 & 4-hole
scissors
Stanley knife
pencils

Post-It pads
glue stick
small screwdriver
spare flip chart pens—varied colours
OHP pens and loose acetates
methylated spirit and tissues (for cleaning acetates and OHP lenses!)
extension cable
video cassette tapes
self-adhesive name tags
ruler

You would be amazed how often such items can be of use on a training course.

Meals and break times form an important part of any course. They can considerably add to the enjoyment and success of the course. Conversely, they can be an inflexible barrier which interferes with the smooth operation of a course and the delegates' learning.

It is important that your requirements are understood by the host establishment and that your group is fully aware of what the arrangements are.

It is advisable to take your coffee, tea and meal breaks outside the conference room so that people have an opportunity to get out. For some it may be their only opportunity to smoke if a no-smoking rule has been applied by the group. It also offers the opportunity for informal interaction with and between course members and helps establish more positive relationships. Breaks may also give you the opportunity to deal with any problems that have arisen, sometimes behind the scenes, so that your own credibility does not suffer.

As for lunch, it is best to try and arrange a light lunch, again out of the conference room and of the self-service variety. A heavy lunch does nothing to prevent drowsiness during the post-lunch session (often called 'the graveyard session') while a lunch reliant upon waiter service can result in lengthy delays, delegate frustration and a late return to the course. Furthermore, if the business of eating is over relatively quickly delegates have the opportunity to walk in the fresh air, or to do something else to relax their mind and make them more ready for the afternoon session.

With regard to the post-lunch session, as a general rule it is often best to make it a practical one rather than a theoretical one and to ensure that the interval between lunch and afternoon tea is not too long. Anything that gets delegates into the participative mode after lunch is usually welcomed.

It is also worth stating here that there is no direct relationship between the amount and quality of learning and the time spent in formal sessions. Most people are all too aware of the high costs of mounting and running a training event and therefore strive to maximize the use of time. Trainers sometimes therefore fall into the trap of running formal sessions until very late in the evening. It is important to give delegates some time to relax and also time to discuss items informally. Many groups have spent long hours in the bar in the evening discussing work or course-related issues, but at their choice and beyond the confines of formal sessions.

The option of a mid-course break on long residential courses should be given. A change of activity or a short opportunity to escape the confines of the host establishment can be very welcome and energizing. Equally, delegates will usually respond to and welcome the opportunity of an early departure on the last day to beat the traffic and get home.

Messages and interruptions

Arrangements must be made beforehand for the collection of messages. It is important that sessions are not interrupted and that people receive messages during break times. Ensure that delegates know the system for the receipt of messages.

It is suggested that contracts are made by course members with regard to contact with work. This is especially important with in-house courses where the temptation to check the in-tray is much stronger. As far as possible, try to persuade people to become 'unavailable' for the duration of the course. You must also abide by the same rules yourself.

Preparing yourself

All the necessary administrative arrangements have been completed and you have given yourself the best possible chance of success in designing the physical learning environment and ensuring that all the administrative arrangements have been made.

If these have been correctly implemented then you have considerably increased your chances of success. There are other things that you can do and can control to increase the chances of success even further:

1 Be smart, clean and well-groomed. This gives a professional appearance. Your image and attire contribute to the atmosphere. There are no hard-and-fast rules on what to wear. Generally, in-house courses have a more formal attire.

At conference centres and hotels more casual dress is often the rule.

It is important to tune-in to the dress code of the organization for which you are providing the training and make the appropriate adjustments. You usually find, certainly off site, that standards become more relaxed once you get under way.

It is always advisable to take some formal attire with you, particularly if there is likely to be a formal dinner during the training event with visiting dignitaries. You may not need such attire, but if you have it you have more options.

2 Strive for a comfortable, relaxed, friendly but positive environment. Some ways in which you can do this are to:

- welcome people
- smile
- be enthusiastic.

3 Be conscious of your body language and that of others. Maintain good eye contact. Smile. Have a good, open posture. Avoid distracting mannerisms. More will be said about this later in the book.

4 Establish your credibility and that of your colleague(s). Never apologize for being there and thereby demean yourself. Equally, do not build up such an aura of expertise that you become unapproachable.

5 Relax. Be yourself. If you appear tense or over-anxious, that will transfer itself to others. Thorough preparation beforehand should give you confidence. In addition you can:

- take a few moments before the event to relax and gather your thoughts;
- breathe deeply and slowly in a short, private session on your own;
- talk to your colleague, particularly if he or she is much more experienced, and if you need support, ask for it since counselling and supporting each other during the training event is a very therapeutic activity and a good confidence booster;
- observe old pros doing their act and copy their good habits, if appropriate. This can be one great benefit of the team-teaching approach.

You may also wish to do regular relaxation exercises at suitable points during a course. There is a variety of books and tapes available on this subject. Try it and if it works for you, use it.

6 Time-keeping. As part of presenting a professional image it is important that prompt starts are made and that the group understands this. If you are prompt and punctual the group will be the same: if you are late and sloppy, the group will follow that trend.

More flexibility should be allowed with regard to finishing times. If the group is engaged in meaningful activity and learning, then let it go. Equally, if it appears that nothing positive will be obtained by prolonging a session to the stated time, finish early or give the delegates a leisure or private study option. There is nothing worse than keeping tired and disinterested delegates chained to their seats at the end of the day for a meaningless activity and frustrating them even more.

Rules relating to time-keeping are established at the start of the course as part of your contract with the group. If you ensure that you keep to the contract, your credibility will be enhanced.

The first meeting— getting acquainted

Whatever the level of course or whatever the level of the participants, each course is a new experience. An element of the unknown exists for everybody, tutor included.

We have looked elsewhere at the impact of the environment upon the learning process and stressed the importance of the appropriate arrangement of furniture so that interaction between tutor and delegates and between delegates themselves can take place freely.

Another important part of the environment is what we can loosely term 'climate'. It is a difficult concept to define, but a positive or negative climate can have an enormous impact upon the learning process.

A climate that is characterized by tenseness, low trust, formality, coldness, aloofness, or is authority orientated, competitive and judgemental *is not* conducive to learning. A climate that is characterized by a relaxed atmosphere, mutual trust and respect, informality, warmth, collaboration and mutual support *is* conducive to learning.

In a nutshell, if participants feel good about themselves and the experience, and if they feel secure and their levels of anxiety are low, then we are well on the way to achieving a positive outcome.

The establishment of such a positive climate is not achieved immediately. One cannot just press a button, as if one were turning on the lights, in order to create the right climate. It needs work, and it starts at the beginning of a course.

In fact, for both tutor and delegate the first meeting or first session is the most crucial. It is the time of getting to know one another, forming impressions and deciding whether to make a commitment. One of the main objectives, if not the main objective, of the first session is to begin the process of getting acquainted so that levels of anxiety can be reduced. It is the first step in the process of climate setting and it is as much for the benefit of the tutor as it is for the delegate.

Many years ago, when I took up my first teaching post in a Secondary school, an old hand took me aside and gave me a little fatherly advice. 'You have to have discipline', he said. 'Until you have got them under control you can't teach them anything.'

For the adult situation the advice could be 'You have to have them feeling secure and relatively free from anxiety, otherwise they will not be in a position to learn.'

Having stated *what* we should do, we then have again to ask *how* should we do it. How should we begin the process of establishing a positive climate and of allaying people's anxieties, including our own? In other words, how should we break the ice?

It is important to devote the first session to breaking the ice and commencing the 'getting acquainted' process (unless, of course, everyone knows everyone else, which is rare).

A number of ice-breaking exercises are now available. It is important to choose one, or devise your own, which is appropriate to the group. A common method that I have used many times is the icebreaker 'Pairs Interviews', sometimes referred to as 'Jack and Jill'. A version of this is reproduced below and can be adapted in several ways.

Pairs Interviews ('Jack and Jill')

Activity outline

This exercise asks the delegates, working in pairs, to informally interview each other and then to introduce their partner to the rest of the group. This exercise is generally more effective if carried out at the start of a course after the tutors have introduced themselves.

Training application

Time allowed: Approx. 5 to 10 minutes for each interview.

Group size: Best suited to groups of 8 to 16 participants.

Space required: A large conference area in which delegates can move their chairs to guarantee some privacy. If adjoining syndicate rooms are available, these should be used.

Materials needed: None.

Trainer administration

1 The trainer begins by *explaining* the need to get to know one another; that, as delegates usually feel more embarrassed talking about themselves than others, each delegate will introduce one person to the group.

2 Delegates are asked to pair off, and if possible choose someone they do not know. (If they are hesitant, the trainer can randomly decide the pairing. Should it be necessary, one group may contain three members.)

3 Each pair is to find a place in which to work with some degree of privacy. The pair are then to spend 5–10 minutes interviewing each other, learning each other's names and sharing information about background, interests, values, goals, etc.

4 The group leader may wish to call out the time when one minute remains so that both partners have an opportunity to share information about themselves.

5 When the allotted time has elapsed, the trainer calls the group together.

6 When the group has assembled, the trainer explains that each person will introduce their partner to the group. Each person is allowed two minutes for the introduction. For example: 'This is Jill. She is a pharmacist and lives here in town. She was born in Edinburgh and graduated at ...', and so on.

7 The trainer asks for a pair to volunteer to begin the introductions. The exercise continues until all the group members have been introduced.

Variations

Delegates talk to the group as if they were their

partner, for example: 'My name is Jill ...'. Or they stand behind their partner's chair for the introduction.

If the members of a group appear to be uninhibited, the group leader can ask the partners to perform the introductions by acting out each other's key characteristics or personal traits.

The trainer can encourage the group members to ask questions about the person who is being introduced. The partner must answer the questions to the best of his or her ability. Then the person being introduced responds as to the accuracy of his or her partner's statements.

NOTE: The variations are numerous, each one requiring a degree of risk-taking on the part of the delegate. It is the role of the trainer to sense what is appropriate for the group in question.

Exercises

1 Consider three different training events in which you have been involved.

   (a) Describe the physical learning environment.
   (b) How did it contribute to the success of the course?
   (c) How did it detract from the success of the course?

2 List some of your feelings in different group situations where the layout was different.

   (a) What have you learned about yourself?
   (b) What can you do in the role of trainer to improve your comfort level?

3 Consider an experienced trainer you have observed.

   (a) How did he or she arrange the environment and use it to enhance learning?
   (b) What did you learn and what could you adopt?

4 How do you feel before a training event? What, if anything, do you do beforehand to combat any anxieties? What has a positive effect? What else could you do to make yourself more relaxed?

5 List three different 'ice-breakers' you have observed.

   (a) Were they successful?
   (b) What were the benefits for yourself (if in the training role) and for the participants?
   (c) List anything you learned from your observations.

Summary

Some of the major points from this chapter are:

- Detailed planning and preparation beforehand increases the chances of success.
- The physical learning environment can have a profound effect upon learning, and considerable thought and attention should be given to the layout.
- The first session is crucial—'ice-breakers' help greatly in getting people interacting and launching the course in a positive way.

Further reading

M. Barca and K. Cobb, *Beginnings and Endings*. Gower, Aldershot, 1994.

S. Bartram and B. Gibson, *Activities for Developing Training Skills*. Gower, Aldershot, 1994.

T. Bourner, V. Martin and P. Race, *Workshops That Work: 100 Ideas to Make your Training Events More Effective*. McGraw-Hill, Maidenhead, 1993.

A. Kirby, *Games for Trainers*. (Vol. 1 and 2.) Gower, Aldershot, 1992.

A. Kirby, *A Compendium of Icebreakers, Energisers and Introductions*. Gower, Aldershot, 1993.

A. Kirby, *Games for Trainers* (Vol. 3.) Gower, Aldershot, 1994.

John W. Newston and Edward E. Scannel, *Games Trainers Play: Experiential Learning Exercises*. McGraw-Hill, San Francisco, 1980.

University Associates, *Encyclopaedia of Icebreakers*. San Diego, California, 1983.

4 Learning theory

It is important that trainers have some knowledge and understanding of the learning process, particularly in the adult. This will help you immensely in both the design and delivery of a course.

At the end of this chapter you will be able to:

- define learning and state its three component parts;
- distinguish between traditional teaching and learner-directed training;
- distinguish between product and process;
- identify and understand some of the main groups of learning theory and how they might be applied in training;
- identify the four stages in the learning cycle;
- list the four major learning styles.

Learning theory has evolved over the last century as a result of numerous experiments that have been conducted, often with animals. Different schools of psychological thinking have made their various contributions to our pool of knowledge. No single theory has obtained complete agreement among psychologists about the details of the learning process, but they all accept the basic premise that learning occurs whenever one adopts new, or modifies existing, behaviour patterns in a way that has some influence on future performance or attitudes.

Learning is not about behaviour changes that occur as a result of the maturation process, but is about a change in behaviour that is reasonably permanent and must grow out of past experience. It follows, therefore, in the case of the adult whose reservoir of experience is so much greater, that any behaviour change must occur as a result of a deeper and more meaningful experience than that of the child. Thus, some of the theories of learning that have been applied to the teaching of children may not be as effective if applied to the teaching of adults. The adult learner is a somewhat different species from the child learner and this should be reflected in the design, method and delivery of a training event.

Harris and Schwahn reiterate that 'Learning is essentially change due to experience', but then go on to distinguish between learning as a product (which explains the end result or outcome of the learning experience), learning as a process (which emphasizes what happens during the course of learning experience in attaining a given learning product or outcome) and learning as a function (which emphasizes certain critical aspects of learning, such as motivation, retention and transfer) which make behavioural changes in human learning possible.

Early learning theories fall into two major categories:

- Behaviourist or Stimulus-Response theories. These include the diverse theories of Thorndike, Pavlov, Skinner and Hull
- Cognitive theories. These include those of Tolman and the *gestalt* psychologists. They tend to deal more with the acquisition of knowledge.

Types of learning can be categorized into three groups:

Cognitive learning. This means knowledge learning. It not only includes the knowledge *per se*, but also what to do with it or how to apply it. Thus the investigative process and the principles of problem solving and decision making are part of this group.

Much learning of this nature is imparted by the lecture method, but can be reinforced by a variety of methods such as private study, process reviews, role plays and case studies.

Psychomotor learning. These are the physiological skills that are required in order to complete a task. Examples would be driving a car or giving an oral presentation.

The most effective environment in which to gain these physical skills is the 'laboratory', in which students actually gain hands-on experience. The lecturer only prepares the students by giving them the knowledge before entering the arena to practise. It is only in the arena that the real learning takes place. This experiential approach is used in the training of airline pilots in simulators.

In no area of learning is the old Chinese proverb more appropriate:

I hear, I forget,
I see, I remember,
I do, I understand.

Affective learning. This is related to attitudes, values and interests and is the most difficult training of all, mainly because it is difficult to measure.

Such changes tend to occur as a result of the training process. They can certainly be influenced by such factors as trainer style, facilitation skills, the learning environment and the learning method. Some of the techniques used in management development or team-building programmes that involve the use of CCTV and psychometric inventories can be very powerful in effecting attitudinal change. Such techniques, however, need a high level of sensitivity and facilitation skills, particularly on the part of the trainer, if they are to have a positive effect. Unskilfully and unprofessionally handled, more harm than good can result.

Groups of learning theory

There is no one unified theory of adult learning. Over the past century there have evolved many theories of learning and a comprehensive overview of all these theories would constitute a book in its own right. Such a detailed review of all these theories is clearly beyond the scope of this book, but for those who wish to study them in more detail, the further reading section at the end of this chapter will serve as a good starting point.

There is no one theory which is the best or has more to recommend it than the others. Learning is a complex process and each theory can have a practical application some of the time. Depending upon your objectives, one theory or group of theories may be more relevant to the design of your training event and influence your methodology. The intention of this chapter is, therefore, to give a brief outline of a number of learning theories that may be relevant. These will include one or two new developments in the field and the intention is not to offer a sound, academic classification of learning theories, but to heighten the reader's awareness of their existence and their possible implications for training.

The following main groups of learning theories will be outlined:

1 Reinforcement (or stimulus–response) theories
2 Cognitive theories
3 A process model of adult learning
4 Experiential learning
5 Learning to learn and self-development
6 Mental processes
7 Emerging horizons

Reinforcement (or stimulus–response) theories

The most famous exponents of this set of theories are Pavlov and Skinner, who carried out numerous experiments with animals. A basic premise of the theories is that individuals' behaviour can be *conditioned* and a key element in this process is *reinforcement*. Pavlov is associated with *classical conditioning* following experimentation with dogs, and Skinner is associated with *operant conditioning* following experimentation with rats and pigeons. The Skinnerian term is derived from the fact that the individual must act or operate on the environment in order to be rewarded (operant behaviour).

Most of Pavlov's work (dated *circa* 1880) was limited to physiological reflex actions, particularly the salivation reflex in dogs. By accident he discovered that dogs would salivate when a previously unconnected stimulus, besides food, was present, provided that on a number of previous occasions the stimulus appeared at or just before the presentation of the food. As a result of this, Pavlov was able to teach dogs to associate salivation with an unconnected stimulus—in the case of the experiments conducted, the sound of a tuning fork. By pairing the sound of a tuning fork with the presentation of meat, the dog could be conditioned, as a result of association, to salivate at the sound of the tuning fork. This is the process of classical conditioning and has limited practical application in the training situation.

Skinner (*circa* 1935) placed hungry rats in boxes containing levers which, when pressed, caused the release of food pellets. Exploratory behaviour by the rats occasionally resulted in a chance contact with a lever. After several accidental lever contacts the rat realized the relationship between pressing the lever and obtaining food. This is trial and error learning in which the rat rewards or reinforces its own behaviour.

When the rat obtained the food pellet every time it pressed the lever, Skinner called it *continuous reinforcement*. When the rat was occasionally rewarded, he called it *intermittent reinforcement*. In the early stages of conditioning, continuous reinforcement is needed to establish the stimulus–response (S–R) link. When the rat is no longer hungry its perseverance wanes and intermittent reinforcement can be introduced, with gradually increasing intervals between each reward.

By using varying schedules of intermittent and continuous reinforcement with food pellets, Skinner taught a pigeon to walk in a figure of eight. Over a short period of time the appropriate movement in either a clockwise or anti-clockwise direction was suitably rewarded.

A modern day and commercial application of operant conditioning can be witnessed in the Sea World amusement parks of California and Florida. One example is an act in which Shamu, a large, killer whale, jumps out of the water to clear a rope—a feat which brings gasps of admiration from large audiences who also ponder 'how do they do that?' The answer is operant conditioning in which good or desirable behaviour by the killer whale is reinforced by the reward of a fish. In the early days of training (or conditioning) a rope is placed under the surface of the water. Every time the whale swims under the rope no reward is offered; every time the whale swims above the rope it is rewarded with a fish. Once the whale has established the connection between the desired behaviour (swimming above the rope) and the reward (a fish), the rope is gradually raised until it is clear of the water. If the whale wants a fish it has to jump clear of the water. From such experiments several valuable conclusions about learning and motivation can be drawn:

1 Each step in the learning process should be short and grow out of previously learned behaviour.
2 In the early stages, learning should be regularly rewarded and all stages carefully controlled by a schedule of continuous and/or intermittent reinforcement.
3 Reward should quickly follow the correct response. This is called *feedback* and is based on the principle that motivation is enhanced when we are informed of our progress. This linked to 1 above because, in order to ensure a high success rate, the steps in the learning process must be small and within the capabilities of the learner.

Operant conditioning has important lessons for both parents and managers in their day-to-day dealings with offspring and subordinates respectively. It also underpins the design of programmed learning and more recent, sophisticated developments in computer-based learning. By receiving positive feedback, learners are encouraged to continue and extend their learning.

Cognitive theories

Many psychologists believe that human behaviour is too complex for simple S–R theories to offer a rational explanation. They believe that something happens internally between stimulus and response, possibly through information processing, and this would explain behaviour. Among the things that might happen are 'understanding', 'thinking', 'reflection', 'analysis of experience', 'memorizing', 'retrieving' or 'remembering'. All of these enable the individual to experience *insight*, which is a key concept of *gestalt* psychology or cognitive theory. Insight occurs when a solution to a problem becomes obvious and is a solution which can be used again in a similar situation or new situations.

The first demonstration of insightful learning was made by Kohler who, in the Canary Islands in the 1920s, experimented with chimpanzees. Bananas were placed at varying distances, out of reach, outside the chimpanzees' cage. A number of short, individual sticks inside the cage could, if slotted together, be used to reach and procure the bananas. Kohler observed that after a period of unproductive exploratory activity, 'the penny dropped' (insight) and the chimpanzees could solve the problem. Further experiments in which bananas were hung from the roof of the cage and individual boxes were strewn around the cage floor produced similar results.

The emphasis, therefore, in *gestalt* psychology is on the adaptability in the use of existing knowledge to form new insights rather than programmed repetition of stimulus–response pairings. It is concerned with the internal processes which we use to recognize and define problems and seek solutions. Solutions can be reached either by trial and error, by deduction, by seeking information and assistance, or by a combination of all three. We see the situation as a whole and begin to make sense of it and recognize it. It is therefore more likely that solutions can be more easily reached by working in groups rather than as solitary individuals—as was the case with Kohler's chimpanzees. Once the methodology and solution(s) have been internalized, transfer of learning to future situations should occur.

Cognitive theories have been applied in a training situation to the technique of discovery learning and problem solving which have equal application for child and adult learners. With this technique the trainee, upon being give a task, has to search and sift clues on how best to progress. A means of unassisted learning through experience is provided that will hopefully lead to the development of insights into key relationships and solutions.

From the trainer's point of view, the design of the task is crucial. On training courses, a number of structured experiences (carefully designed tasks which will produce a specific outcome and therefore learning) can be used. In developing new ones it is essential that they are piloted several times to ensure that they achieve their objectives.

A process model of adult learning

It was only after the Second World War that serious enquiry really began into adult learning and development. Most of this early research took place in the USA.

At the same time, in Europe, the concept of a unified theory of adult learning had been evolving for which the term *andragogy* was used to differentiate it from the theory of youth learning, *pedagogy*. This term was used by Malcolm Knowles in his work of developing a unified system of adult learning. It is essentially a *process* model and is based around the premise that, as individuals mature, their need and capacity to be self-directing, to utilize their experience in learning, to identify their own readiness to learn, and to organize their learning around life problems, increases steadily from infancy to pre-adolescence and then increases rapidly during adolescence.

If the culture of the institution or social system, such as a school or family unit, denies or negates the need and ability to be self-directing, then the result is tension, resistance, resentment and even rebellion in the individual. Motivational theorists need look no further for many of the problems that exist today in our schools and colleges.

Andragogical theory is based on the following four assumptions that distinguish it from pedagogy or traditional teaching methods:

1 Concept of the learner.
2 Role of learner's experience.

3 Readiness to learn.
4 Orientation to learning.

A more detailed comparison of the two approaches with regard to the four different assumptions is given in Table 4.1.

Table 4.1   *Pedagogy v. Andragogy*

With regard to	Pedagogy	Andragogy
Concept of the learner	Role of learner is dependent	Role of learner is essentially self-directing
	Teacher takes responsibility for the whole learning process	Role of teacher is to encourage and nurture this self-directed need
Role of learners' experience	Learners bring little experience to the learning situation	Learners' experience accumulated over a lifetime is a great resource for learning both for self and others
	Learners dependent on 'expert' input	Learners attach greater significance to what they experience rather than what they are told
	Main techniques are transmittal techniques	Main techniques are experiential techniques
Readiness to learn	Learners learn what they are conditioned to learn to obtain parental, societal approval	Learners learn when they feel a need to learn
	Fear of failure is a great motivator	Learning should meet their needs to help them cope with the demands of their world—home, work, etc.
	Learning is standardized and progressive because it is aimed at the same age group and every age group is similar in its learning needs and its readiness to learn	Learning should be organized to meet learner needs and sequenced according to individual's ability and readiness to learn

With regard to	Pedagogy	Andragogy
Orientation to learning	Learning is subject-oriented, with emphasis on content, most of which they may forget because it has no immediate relevance (principle of 'deferred gratification')	Learners seek to acquire competence to cope with demands of their world; they seek personal development and achievement of potential; they also seek immediate gratification; learning must be relevant and immediately applicable

Source: Malcolm S. Knowles, *The Modern Practice of Adult Education: from pedagogy to androgogy*, © 1980, pp 43–44. Reprinted by permission of Prentice-Hall, Inc., Englewood Cliffs, New Jersey.

Implications for the trainer:

1 Motivation of the individual is an intrinsic process (the 'push' from within, which is self-generated), so that they are self-directing. The role of the trainer is to create a learning environment that harnesses these intrinsic drives and not an environment that suppresses them. An informal environment is best. Formality can create tension and tension impedes learning.

2 Self-directing individuals occasionally need support. The role of the trainer is to recognize when this exists and provide the appropriate support, either personally or using group members.

3 Whenever possible the experience of each individual must be tapped. To deny a person's experience is to deny that person. The probing of experience from people with different backgrounds so that they may learn from each other is one of the fundamentals of Action Learning which has been applied with notable success in problem-solving situations in industry and is now being used as the basic methodology on management development programmes up to and including the MBA.

4 The participative method should be widely used on training programmes because:
   (a) it utilizes members' experience for the benefit of others, including the trainer;
   (b) it is only by having an experience that people begin the experiential learning cycle which is outlined later on;
   (c) involvement in an experience ensures that the span of attention is widened so the participants learn more;
   (d) by participation in an experience, participants not only gain knowledge and skill, but also have certain feelings and emotions

that can be a powerful way of changing attitudes and can give them greater self-insight and greater insight into others.

5 The content of a programme should be a contract between trainer and learner. This meets the learner's needs for relevance to the present and moves away from the principle of deferred gratification, which is unacceptable for most adults. The involvement of the learner in deciding programme content also increases commitment because they part-own the decision.

6 Where knowledge is imparted with the delegate in the passive mode, there should be ample opportunity to reinforce the learning by varying methods. Reinforcement is a vital part of the learning process and methods used should vary according to subject material and individual learning styles. Variety stimulates and makes the learner more receptive.

To summarize, according to Knowles, the andragogical model is a *process model, not a content model* that has been employed by traditional education. The andragogical tutor is a facilitator, a consultant, a change agent, who prepares in advance a set of procedures for involving the learners in a process of:

1 establishing a climate conducive to learning;
2 creating a mechanism for mutual planning;
3 diagnosing the needs for learning;
4 formulating objectives and therefore content which will satisfy these needs;
5 designing a pattern of learning experiences;
6 conducting these learning experiences with suitable techniques and materials;
7 evaluating the learning outcomes and rediagnosing learning needs.

The process model does not ignore content—rather the emphasis is on providing procedures and resources for facilitating the learner's acquisition of information and skills. This ownership by the delegate of the programme objectives and content increases commitment, harnesses their intrinsic motivation and is a powerful way of influencing attitudinal change. If it only serves to influence their attitude to training and make it more positive, that in itself is a powerful achievement.

Experiential learning theory

This relatively recent theory has much in common with other theories, e.g. cognitive theories, and has its roots in laboratory training and T-groups. It puts the emphasis on the actual experiences that people go through as the starting point for the learning process and then emphasizes the analytical mental processes that individuals use to analyse the experience. Feelings are also part of any experience which, if explored and analysed, can help increase self-insight. In short, experience when allied to analysis can bring about behavioural change.

The model is not only an important theory of learning but is extremely useful as a means of explaining individual differences in learning style. In the 1970s David Kolb developed the Experiential Learning Cycle, stating that there are four distinct stages in the learning process and that each individual has a preference for a particular style of learning.

Kolb developed his experiential learning theory, seeing it as an integrated process in four main stages:

1 Learning begins with a 'here and now' experience. This could conform to existing views or contradict them.
2 This experience is followed by a collection of data and observations or reflections about that experience.
3 A continuation stage with an analysis of the data, when we begin to conceptualize and commence the internalization process of what has been learnt from the experience.
4 The final stage when we modify or alter our behaviour. At this stage we enter a stage of experimentation and test the new knowledge or concepts to see if they work in practice.

Kolb's circular learning pattern is shown in Figure 4.1. When one 'revolution' has been completed, the cycle begins again.

Kolb developed beyond his theory arguing '... as a result of our hereditary equipment, our particular past life experience and the demands of our present environment, most people develop learning styles that emphasize some learning abilities over others'. He then

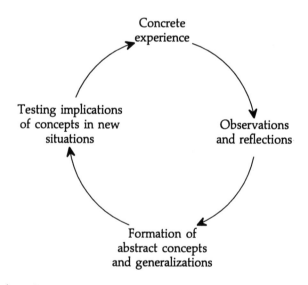

Figure 4.1   *The Learning Cycle—Kolb*
Source: 'Towards an applied theory of experiential learning', in *Theories of Group Process* by D. A. Kolb and R. Fry © Wiley, 1975. Reprinted by permission of John Wiley & Sons Ltd.

developed a Learning Style Inventory in order to measure an individual's relative emphasis on each of the four learning abilities. He named the four basic styles *converger, diverger, assimilator* and *accommodator*.

An alternative description of learning styles was produced, along with a questionnaire, by Peter Honey and Alan Mumford in 1983 (2nd edn. 1986). They described the four basic styles as *activist, theorist, reflector* and *pragmatist*, each one largely corresponding to each of the four stages in their learning cycle. The emphasis is on preference in the way an individual learns, which could have significant implications in the design and methodology used on training and development programmes. Furthermore, it is not believed that one's preferences are incapable of change—basic style can change but requires, first, self-awareness of one's strengths and weaknesses and, second, a commitment to change. Whereas the responsibility for the former rests with the trainer, responsibility for the latter rests firmly with the learner. An ability to develop one's weaker styles of learning can result in a significant level of personal development for many individuals. (A more detailed description of Honey and Mumford's four learning styles, along with their learning cycle, is given in Chapter 5.)

A good example of how the theory can be applied is in learning how to improve at a sport such as cricket, golf or tennis. The trainee is likely to go round the learning cycle many times, using a variety of methods such as individual tuition, demonstration and coaching, practice, reading, watching others, receiving feedback from a video, reflecting and analysing his or her game and playing in a competitive situation. Such a variety of training methods will take the individual around the learning cycle many times over, which will reinforce earlier learning.

While the trainer can utilize the Learning Styles questionnaire to determine the composition of the group, it must be remembered that it will offer no guarantee of successful group learning. Other variables, such as interaction among group members and facilitation style, can have a significant impact on determining whether learning outcomes are positive or negative. Nevertheless, such an instrument can be invaluable in increasing individual self-awareness and also in helping the trainer to choose the appropriate training method.

Experiential learning theory underpins a method now increasingly used in management training, namely Action Learning. This method was pioneered by Revans with such organizations as the National Coal Board and GEC, and it utilizes the group as a resource for solving real life, work-related problems. Individuals (called 'fellows') form a group ('set') to address and solve problems and implement solutions. Such sets usually run for a minimum of six months and have attached to them an external facilitator, or set adviser, whose primary role is to offer an expert input of knowledge in an academic discipline relevant to the project in order to help the set focus on the key issues and guide the set appropriately towards project completion.

Thus, both end product (outcome) and process are important learning vehicles for participants and make significant contributions to an individual's capacity to learn how to learn.

Learning to learn and self-development

The recently emerging trend away from teaching to learning has gathered increasing momentum. Consequently attention has focused more and more on how to equip the learner with the strategies and range of learning styles that are appropriate not only for present learning but also are transferable to future learning situations. Individuals must recognize that opportunities for learning are all around them and that experience needs to be fully utilized and processed.

Learning is not a static or one-off event. It is a continuous process and we need to know what to do, how to do it and when to act—and part of that process is adapting new strategies and strengthening existing styles, however weak. Learning to learn, therefore, is at the very heart of self-development.

Two definitions of 'Learning to Learn' will help clarify the concept further. First, Mumford defines the four major elements as:

- Helping managers to know the stages of the learning process and blockages to learning.
- Helping managers to understand their own preferred approaches to learning.
- Assisting individuals in making the best use of their existing learning preferences, or building additional strengths and overcoming blockages.
- Helping individuals to carry their understanding of learning from off-the-job to on-the-job opportunities.

Second, Smith defines Learning to Learn as: 'possessing or acquiring the knowledge and skills to learn effectively in whatever learning situation one encounters.' However, he does stress that there is probably no such thing as a 'complete learner', e.g. someone may be effective when learning independently, yet be ineffective in the classroom.

Opportunities for learning are probably greater now than ever before. In addition to learning from everyday experience, the opportunities provided by new technology, such as computer-assisted programs, are enormous.

It would probably be useful at this point to describe briefly the work of Allen Tough at the Ontario Institute of Education. His research in 1970 revealed that the typical adult conducts about eight learning projects in one year and that the average person spends about 100 hours per project or 800 hours every year.

It may well be that the number of hours devoted to learning projects will have increased since 1970, given the increased commitment of organizations and managers to continued development and the need for constant retraining and updating because of the ever-increasing pace of change. It is important that adults optimize their learning from this time commitment, whatever the commitment. Learning how to learn is vital to the success of this process. Confidence in learning breeds competence in learning and is a great motivator to future learning. Furthermore, both individuals and organizations need to look beyond the present and to the future, and individuals need to be empowered to take responsibility for their learning as part of a continual process of development.

Mental processes

New technology has made a great contribution to our understanding of the brain. Sophisticated equipment, such as brain scanners, has increased our understanding of the physiology and functioning of various areas of the brain. This section will look at memory and outline the different functions of the two hemispheres of the brain. It is also becoming clear that the potential of the brain is almost unlimited and that we only use a fraction of that potential. The number of possible combinations, interconnections and thought processes in the brain probably exceeds the number of atoms in the universe! By utilizing our knowledge of learning and a number of new techniques, we can begin to make greater use of that potential.

Memory

This term is usually used to describe the activities of acquiring, retaining and recalling information at any time. It has been viewed as a faculty capable of being exercised and improved, rather like a muscle, in order to improve the quantity and quality of what we learn.

Several kinds of memory exist:

- Visual—it is this aspect of memory that those possessing a photographic memory exercise
- Auditory
- Kinaesthetic—this refers to movement memory and would be utilized in sport, touch-typing or any activity requiring muscle coordination.

When we use our memory the process of recovery is called *remembering*.

We have two types of memory (irrespective of the kind of memory): short-term memory and long-term memory.

Short-term memory (STM)
This is a temporary store of a small amount of information. Information entering the STM is either quickly lost or transferred to the long-term memory (LTM).

The STM has a very limited capacity. As a rule of thumb, we can recall seven items—objects, letters, numbers, arranged at random. For example, write the following sequence of numbers on a flip chart and ask a group to remember them. If successful, after each group, move on to the next group. See how far you get.

Try	1367
Then try	14859
Then try	278643
Then try	78563142
Then try	836723195

You can improve this skill in one of two ways:

- by the process of 'chunking' which involves grouping items into chunks numbering no more than seven. The technique is widely used in learning subjects like typing or morse when items (dots, dashes, letters) are brought together and learned in groups.
- by arranging items in a meaningful way. The following two exercises exemplify this.

Exercise 1   Write the following list of numbers on a flip chart, give the group 20 seconds to memorize the list and then invite them to remember it.

7142128354249566370778849198.

The delegates will not be able to recall this sequence unless they realize that it is the seven times table, which will facilitate recall.

Exercise 2   Write the following sentences individually on a flip chart. Give the group 20 seconds to memorize each sentence and invite them to write it down.

LPB ODN QRX GKT KRZ UCF JMA ISW

THE BIG FAT CAT SAT ON THE MAT

The implication of this exercise for the trainer is that meaning assists memory and we can remember very little of what we do not understand.

This addition of meaning is the main reason for the use of *mnemonics* which are extremely useful in examinations. Provided there are not too many of them, they are a most useful aid to memory. Two examples will serve to show their use and both arise out of helping my own children while at school taking public examinations.

Example 1   Ask students to recite in chronological order the main geological time periods from the Cambrian to the Pleistocene. While they may be familiar with most of the periods, they will probably not be able to name the sequence correctly. Equip them with the mnemonic 'China Owls Seldom Deceive Clay Pigeons, They Just Chase Each Other Making Preposterous Puns' and it becomes much easier. The first letter of each word in the sentence is the first letter of a geological period, the names of which the students will become very familiar with.

Example 2 Ask students to list the ten minerals in order of hardness from talc to diamond. The mnemonic 'The Girl Can Flirt And Other Queer Things Can Do' makes memorizing them much easier. Students will be familiar with the names of each of the minerals through practical, hands-on experience.

Recall is facilitated by rehearsal such as rote learning. Those of us who repeated our multiplication tables in our formative years or who regularly use a telephone number are often capable of impressive acts of memory. The more the cycle is repeated, the more likely the information is to pass to the long-term store. There probably lurks in our LTM many a telephone number, car registration number, post or zip code, capable of being recalled following regular usage in the distant past.

Long-term memory (LTM) Usually information lodged here is more permanent and the process of transfer from the STM to the LTM is assisted by revision or repetition. Also, the less the distraction or interference during a session of learning, the more chance that the information will be committed to long-term memory. The following quotation from Dale aptly summarizes the situation:

> ... for material to enter long term storage it has to survive an initial period during which retention loss can be extremely rapid. In order to survive, the amount of material should be small; it should be as free as possible from inter-item acoustic confusions, it should be varied so that interference between successive messages is minimised; also an opportunity for a brief period of silent rehearsal should be provided after each component message is presented.

There are three essential processes in the long-term memory:

1 **Encoding**: the process of passing information from STM to the LTM. It is probable that the information passes through several levels of processing such as visual/auditory, syntactic and semantic, to be stored in either non-verbal imagery or in verbal syntactic form.
2 **Storage**: the capacity of the memory is enormous, especially when we consider the amount of information and experience we utilize every day.
3 **Retrieval**: information stored in the memory is retrieved when appropriate as part of the process of remembering, and often in great detail. Whether anything committed to the LTM is ever completely forgotten is, for the moment, unclear. Occasionally, something lodged deep in the LTM resurfaces after a trigger or stimulus.

Visualization   Research has now revealed that the brain has two distinct halves which have different functions and very different ways of processing information. The two halves are linked by the *corpus collosum* which is also used to send messages from one side of the brain to the other. While the two halves do function together, research with patients in whom the link was severed revealed the two halves can function separately, without communication with each other.

The specializations of the two sides of the brain are shown in Figure 4.2. It is not yet certain how the two halves are coordinated. Neither half has a monopoly of a particular cognitive style, the functions being mainly degrees of emphasis. There are implications arising from this phenomenon for the trainer:

- An awareness of this split in brain function, and of one's own strengths and weaknesses, is required.
- It is possible to develop the weaker half of the brain. There are a number of techniques and exercises which can be used to develop both sides and brain interaction, which can constitute a self-development project. Most of us tend to have a stronger or more well-developed half and very few of us can claim the complete development and effective use and coordination of both halves.

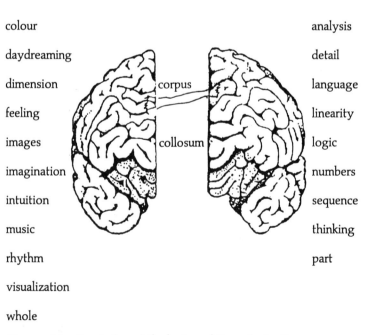

RIGHT	LEFT
colour	analysis
daydreaming	detail
dimension	language
feeling	linearity
images	logic
imagination	numbers
intuition	sequence
music	thinking
rhythm	part
visualization	
whole	

Figure 4.2 *Front view of the brain and its main functions*

So-called geniuses like Einstein and Leonardo da Vinci are often quoted as good examples of people with well-developed left and right brains.

- The trainer should attempt to utilize both brain hemispheres of delegates on courses and in other training activities. Thus case studies using logical interpretation, along with visual aids, imagery and sensory stimuli which will appeal to the right side of the brain, should be used to enhance the impact of the message and achieve greater internalization.

Emerging horizons

In this final section, two new developments will be summarized briefly.

Accelerated Learning

Rose (1991) suggests that the average human being uses only four per cent of his or her potential brain power, saying that in many Westernized countries we have inherited a culturally-imposed legacy of limiting individual learning and development. Much of this is a result of the way we are taught to learn in the school system. The main emphasis is on developing left-brain functions through verbal and deductive subject content. In addition, in organizational life and in society, we tend to place higher value on logical and analytical thinking rather than intuitive and artistic ability. Independence of thought and creativity are not usually given high recognition. We thus starve the right side of the brain of development and, therefore, limit the whole brain's potential.

Accelerated Learning methods attempt to stimulate the whole brain, not just one hemisphere and emphasize the role played by our emotional state in learning because it produces a higher state of arousal, thereby increasing the chances of retention. Also, if we feel good, we are more receptive to inputs through the various sensory pathways. To make use of the whole brain, there is a need not only for logical thought but also for imagery, as visual association assists memory.

With Accelerated Learning techniques, use is made of a variety of sensory pathways—visual, auditory, kinaesthetic, participation and doing. Thus in helping an individual to learn a foreign language, the learning material provides visual aids (books), auditory aids (cassettes) and encouragement to imitate various physical actions or gestures demonstrated in an accompanying video—vocalization is also encouraged by all media. In short, total involvement of the individual and both sides of the brain are utilized and encouraged wherever possible.

Neuro-Linguistic Programming (NLP)

This new development followed work in the USA in the 1970s by a linguistics specialist, Grinder, and a mathematician, Bandler (1979). They made a comprehensive study of excellent practitioners in interpersonal communication, and then identified the key factors contributing to this personal excellence and produced a model for one-to-one communication to assist others (combining skills of mathematical notation and linguistic analysis).

NLP is now increasingly being used in education, training and development. In addition, more recent work by Dilts (1983) and Grinder extended the scope of NLP to leadership and the management of groups and organizations. NLP states that an individual's concept of reality is their own subjective interpretation as the mind acts as a filtering mechanism. Each individual's interpretation is influenced by their experiences and attitudes relating to other people and the world around them. From birth, every individual learns to programme their reactions and develop strategies which become internalized and are lodged in the unconscious mind, and then become automatic. There are two kinds of strategies:

- those involving language;
- those relating to body movement.

By studying excellent performers, the researchers developed a framework to help an individual identify their own strategies and those of others. In short, it helps increase self-awareness and awareness of other strategies. From heightened self-awareness, an individual can choose whether to continue with present automatic responses and behaviours or begin a process of change.

NLP uses many different techniques, some of which relate to self-management. An example of this is 'outcome thinking', which requires the subject to go through a number of stages:

- Thinking of a positive outcome associated with a certain situation and continually rehearsing it by imagining it through as many senses as possible.
- Identifying the personal resources, such as confidence, required to bring about a positive outcome and to find those resources using stimulus–response techniques. The S–R techniques require the individual to think of a time when he or she possessed the required resource, to relive the emotions experienced then and to recall how that state was achieved in order to help recreate it.
- Rehearsing the use of the required resources in the new situation to try and ensure a positive outcome.

Such techniques have been used by sportsmen and women, either to help to achieve success or to avoid getting embroiled in future on-field troubles. For example, soccer players with a short temper, who have been dismissed from the field for retaliating to verbal and physical provocation, are asked to visualize alternative responses in order to avoid future trouble. Trainers also could use this technique to improve their own performance in the many areas associated with delivering or facilitating training.

It can be seen that in the past 100 years our knowledge and understanding of the learning process has increased enormously. No one theory can adequately explain the complex processes of learning in all situations. Furthermore, more than one theory of learning is often applicable in a single situation. Many of the more recent developments in the field incorporate some of the work of the early, learning theorists.

Exercises

1 Consider two good and two poor learning experiences.

    (a) Why were they good?
    (b) Why were they bad?
    (c) What did you learn from them in terms of the principles of adult learning?
    (d) From your answers to these questions, how can you apply your learning points to your own training events?

2 Consider each of the groups of learning theories which have been outlined in this chapter. From your own experience can you:

    (a) think of a situation when it formed the basis of the learning strategy?
    (b) evaluate whether it was effective in helping the trainer meet his or her objectives?

3 Consider a number of training situations in which you might be involved in the near future. Which learning theory or group of theories should influence your design of the training situation?

4 For each of the groups of learning theories described, consider situations when they should be key influences on the training method employed.

Summary

Some of the major points from this chapter are as follows:

- There are three major types of learning which bring about a change in behaviour: cognitive (knowledge), psychomotor (physical skills) and affective (attitudes and values).
- Adults learn very differently from children and the training methods must take account of these differences.
- Participative learning, with the emphasis on process, is becoming more widely recognized and used, and differs greatly in its approach from traditional education.
- People have different styles of learning which should be recognized in course design.
- The adult's self-directing need to learn shows that many people seek learning opportunities beyond the confines of a formal course.
- In the years ahead individuals will need to be empowered to learn how to learn.

- Repetition and reinforcement are important parts of the learning process.
- People can improve the retentive and creative capacities of the brain by using a number of well tried and tested techniques.

Further reading

H. Alder, *The Right Brain Manager*. Piatkus, London, 1993.

H. Alder, *NLP: The New Art and Science of Getting What You Want*. Piatkus, London, 1994.

R. Bandler and J. Grinder, *Frogs into Princes*. Real People Press, London, 1979.

H. C. Dale, 'Memory and effective instruction', *Aspects of Education*, 7, 8–21, 1968.

R. Dilts, *Applications of Neuro-Linguistic Programming*. Meta Publications, Cupertino, California, 1983.

T. L. Harris and W. E. Schwahn, *Selected Readings on the Learning Process*. Oxford University Press, New York, 1961.

P. Honey and A. Mumford, *A Manual of Learning Styles*. Peter Honey, Maidenhead, 1982.

P. Honey and A. Mumford, *Using Your Learning Styles* (2nd edn). Peter Honey, Maidenhead, 1986.

S. Inglis, *Making the Most of Action Learning*. Gower, Aldershot, 1994.

M. S. Knowles, *Self-Directed Learning*. Association Press/Follett, Chicago, 1975.

M. S. Knowles, *The Modern Practice of Adult Education: From Pedagogy to Andragogy*. Follett, Chicago, 1980.

M. S. Knowles, *The Adult Learner: A Neglected Species* (3rd edn). Gulf Publishing Co., Texas, 1984.

W. Kohler, *The Mentality of Apes*. International Library of Psychology, Routledge, London, 1973.

D. A. Kolb, *Experiential Learning*. Prentice Hall, Englewood Cliffs, New Jersey, 1984.

D. A. Kolb and R. Fry, 'Towards an applied theory of experiential learning', in *Theories of Group Process*. (C.L. Cooper, ed.) Wiley, New York, 1975.

I. McGill and L. Beaty, *Action Learning: A Practitioner's Guide*. Kogan Page, London, 1992.

D. Megginson and M. Pedler, *Self Development: A Facilitator's Guide*. McGraw-Hill, Maidenhead, 1992.

A. Mumford, *Making Experience Pay*. McGraw-Hill, Maidenhead, 1980.

A. Mumford, 'Learning to Learn for Managers', *Journal of European Industrial Training*. Vol. 10, No. 2. MCB University Press, Bradford, 1986.

J. O'Connor and J. Seymour, *Introducing Neurolinguistic Programming*. HarperCollins, London, 1990.

M. Pedler, *Action Learning in Practice* (2nd edn). Gower, Aldershot, 1991.

R. W. Revans, *Developing Effective Managers.* Longman, Harlow, 1971.

R. W. Revans, *The Origins and Growth of Action Learning.* Chartwell Bratt, Bromley, 1982.

R. W. Revans, *ABC of Action Learning.* Chartwell Bratt, Bromley, 1983.

C. Rogers, *Freedom to Learn.* Merrill, Columbus, Ohio, 1983.

C. Rose, *Accelerated Learning.* Accelerated Learning Systems Ltd, Aylesbury, 1991.

B. F. Skinner, *Science and Human Behaviour,* Macmillan, New York, 1953.

B. F. Skinner, *Beyond Freedom and Dignity.* Knopf, New York, 1972.

R. Smith, *Learning How to Learn: Applied Theory for Adults.* Open University Press, Milton Keynes, 1984.

A. Tough, *The Adults' Learning Projects. A Fresh Approach to Theory and Practice* (2nd edn). The Ontario Institute for Studies in Education, Toronto, Ontario, 1979.

5 Course members

Any course is sure to be composed of a wide variety of individuals.

At the end of this chapter you will be able to:

- identify a range of expectations of individuals;
- identify several theories of motivation and state several things that motivate people;
- list four major styles of learning;
- consider the above information and how it can influence the design of your training course.

Expectations

Whatever the level of involvement in training or educating adults, one thing can be guaranteed: you will be faced with a heterogeneous group. Part of your task is to mould this heterogeneous unit into an effective and working group so that they go away having learned something and in a positive frame of mind.

When one analyses the heterogeneity of the group in such terms as intelligence level, motivation, skill, experience, culture, etc., one wonders how any group can ever become an effective unit—the task facing the facilitator is daunting and sometimes appears overwhelming.

The task of welding a heterogeneous group into an effective learning unit is one of the great challenges and this is why, when success is achieved, training and working with adults is such a rewarding and stimulating experience.

Some of the individual differences that exist (e.g. motivation) will be discussed later. It is the role of the trainer to be aware of these. It is also the role of the trainer to have some awareness of the delegates' expectations and here there are some common elements.

1 **They often expect to be taught in the old-fashioned way.**
Many attendees are prisoners of their early educational experience. They are steeped in the old-fashioned, forceful and rigid methods. They view the educational process as something that must be endured. If they are actually enjoying it, then they feel guilty.

Many years ago I ran a short course entitled 'Introduction to

Psychology'. Free from the constraints of an examination syllabus and in receipt of feedback from the students on the topics that were of interest, I designed and delivered a programme. Experiential, participative methodology was widely used; 'chalk and talk' was kept to a minimum. The rate of fall-out was small and, towards the end of the course, the participants enquired as to the possibility of a follow-up. We sat down to discuss it and it was then that one middle-aged lady asked me, 'Are we going to be doing some serious work, or are we going to carry on just messing about?'! She had enjoyed the course but felt guilty that she hadn't endured the process.

As a postscript to this anecdote, a follow-up course was designed and delivered; the middle-aged lady attended and we continued to 'mess about'. And everybody enjoyed it!

2 **They expect the trainer to display the appropriate professionalism.**
Attendees expect appropriateness in several areas:

(a) *Knowledge of the subject.* Unless you really are, you are not expected to be the world's greatest authority, but some form of expertise is expected. And if you don't know the answer, ask the group—one of them may know.
(b) *Knowledge of, and possession of some skills in, teaching and facilitation.* With the vast range of learning methods available, no one expects you to be totally at ease with all of them. Know your strengths and your weaknesses, and make the appropriate adjustments.
(c) *Standard of dress.* A sloppy image and appearance do not portray a professional person. I am not advocating the wearing of formal dress, but one can dress smartly without being formal. It is in this area that appropriateness is important. If one is delivering a management training course in-house, then some formal attire is usually the order of the day; if the course is delivered away from base, then smart, casual dress seems to be *de rigeur*. Appropriate dress is one aspect of the norms that a group sets itself and the trainer has to be aware of it and give it consideration in deciding what is appropriate.

It is amazing what delegates observe about trainers and one should never underestimate this, as the following anecdote reveals.

One of the problems in our household is that we have a washing machine that devours socks. It is very discriminating, because it only devours one sock in every pair so that at the end of a week I can be left with numerous socks that don't match.

On a trip to a Mill Shop in the north of England, I discovered a large consignment of plain, fawn-coloured socks. They were on sale at 5p a pair and so, with an eye for a bargain, I duly bought 20 pairs. I reasoned that not only would they colour-match most of my casual attire, but they would also defeat the avaricious appetite of the household washing machine, because they were all the same. No longer would I be left with a pile of socks that didn't match.

At this time I was delivering a 'Train the Trainers' course which met every Friday evening for three hours for three months. I wore casual attire that I felt was appropriate to the informality of the group sessions.

On the last evening of the course it was agreed that we would finish with a wine and cheese function. As this was a little more formal I decided to dispense with my casual attire for the evening and wear a navy blazer, and collar and tie.

At the end of the session, we adjourned to the corner to begin the eating. As I poured the wine for the participants, one turned to the other and said, 'Good Lord. He's at last changed his socks!'

Moral: Nothing goes unnoticed!

3 **They expect to be made to work.**   This counters the strong belief of those who think that participants attend for a social reason or that they will stay away if taxed.

People come to learn and if they are not stretched they will usually vote 'with their feet'. On management development programmes it is often perceived that delegates are going off for a rest. This could not be further from the truth. While there is no denying that the facilities and hospitality of modern-day conference centres are a source of enjoyment, they are usually a source of refreshment and mental replenishment at the end of a long day. If the course menu is not relevant and well presented, the delegates—who are only too aware of the costs to the company of attending programmes—will go back to work.

4 **They expect to be treated with dignity.**   Participants expect to be treated in a dignified and respectful manner. They do not expect to be talked down to. They expect to be treated as equals, although they will respect the role, and therefore group leadership, of the tutor. While that is brought with them, such respect and trust has to be earned by the tutor.

Adults are as vulnerable as children—they dislike harsh criticism, humiliation, neglect and patronage. This vulnerability is derived from the fact that they want their 'adulthood' to be recognized. If adverse feedback has to be given, it should be done on a one-to-one basis in private and should focus not on the person, but on the behaviour of that person. (For more detail, see Chapter 6.)

Motivation

It is important, before looking at some theories of motivation, that a distinction be made between 'intrinsic' and 'extrinsic' motivation.

Intrinsic motivation is the internal drives that an individual experiences (the 'push' from within, which is self-generated). Extrinsic motivation is concerned with incentives (objects external to ourselves which act as a 'pull' from without).

In the training situation, some of the factors that could affect an individual's level of extrinsic motivation are trainer style, learning environment, learning methods, individual and group support, praise, recognition, etc. If one accepts the belief that the adult is strongly self-directing in his or her desire to learn, then the role of the trainer is merely to harness that intrinsic need. The extrinsic, motivating methods do not 'switch on' the learner—they either 'switch off' or increase the drive.

In many human situations—at work, at school, in dressing rooms, etc.—one often hears the phrase 'How do I motivate my people?'. Unfortunately there is no panacea—every situation and every individual must be treated differently. Numerous theories have been propounded on this subject, of which the most common are:

Hierarchy of Needs (Maslow) 1954
Hierarchy of Needs (Alderfer) 1972
Socially Acquired Motives (McClelland et al.) 1976
Two-factor Theory of Work Motivation (Hertzberg) 1966
Theory X and Theory Y (McGregor) 1960
Expectancy Theory (Vroom) 1964

These theories of motivation are all aimed at the occupational field and are included in the content of numerous management development programmes.

It is not the intention here to describe all the models in detail. Countless books have been written on the subject, and any reference library will have them.* Rather the intention is to outline two of the theories: those of Maslow and McClelland.

These have been chosen because they have a more direct relevance to the training situation than the others. In a learning situation, everyone has a variety of needs and most of these needs are covered by the theories of Maslow and McClelland. The trainer must be aware of these needs, and must understand the implications for the training situation. An exercise focusing on how we, as trainers, can meet those needs follows after the outline of the two theories.

* A comprehensive outline of the main theories of motivation is included in Chapter 4, 'Motivation At Work' of *Behavioural Sciences for Managers* (2nd edn). Arnold, London, 1988, by A. G. Cowling, M. J. K. Stanworth, R. D. Bennett, J. Curran and P. Lyons.

Maslow's hierarchy of needs

Maslow stated that every human being has certain *basic* human needs and he arranged them in an order, a hierarchy (see Figure 5.1), with the needs becoming more human as one proceeds up the hierarchy, or up the pyramid, as shown in the diagram. Maslow distinguished the basic needs in the order of their importance (prepotency), so physiological needs must be satisfied before safety needs which, in turn, must be satisfied before love needs, and so on. Progress through the hierarchy, is more likely once the important basic needs have been satisfied as gratification of a need usually leads to the emergence of a higher need.

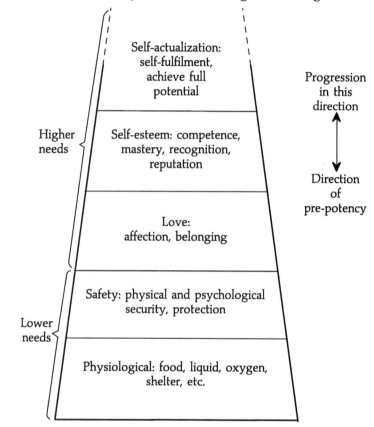

Self-actualization:
self-fulfilment,
achieve full
potential

Higher needs

Self-esteem: competence,
mastery, recognition,
reputation

Love:
affection, belonging

Safety: physical and psychological
security, protection

Lower needs

Physiological: food, liquid, oxygen,
shelter, etc.

Progression
in this
direction

Direction
of
pre-potency

Figure 5.1 *Maslow's hierarchy of basic needs*
Source: *Motivation and Personality*, 2nd edn, by Abraham H. Maslow © 1954 Harper & Row Publishers Inc., © 1970 Abraham H. Maslow. Reprinted with permission of the publisher.

The main divisions of the hierarchy are as follows:

1 **Physiological needs.** The basic needs of the human being are for food, liquid, oxygen, warmth, shelter, etc. They do not include sexual needs as sex is seen as more important to the survival of the species than to the survival of the individual.

2 **Safety needs**. These are higher needs than physiological needs. People need security and safety from threatening objects, or situations. These needs are most evident in young children whose development is generally helped by a stable home background and undisruptive routine.

3 **Love needs**. These only assert themselves when physiological and safety needs have been gratified. Most human beings need both to receive and give affection. They also need to belong (sometimes called the 'herd instinct'), which in turn satisfies their safety needs. In a group situation people can often be made to conform because of a possible threat of isolation, while in society people who do not conform to the 'norms' of behaviour risk being labelled 'drop-outs' and pressure to conform can be quite intense.

4 **Self-esteem needs**. These exist at two levels:

   (a) Desire for competence, achievement, independence, *confidence in oneself* in front of others, etc.
   (b) Desire for prestige, status, recognition, importance, *appreciation by others*.

5 **Self-actualization needs**. The desire to fulfil one's potential ('What a man *can* be, he *must* be'). Self-actualization is dependent on self-realization, because we need to know what we can do before we know if we are doing it correctly.

Linked with basic needs but forming their own hierarchy, are what are termed the *cognitive* needs. The search for knowledge (curiosity needs) and the understanding of that knowledge so that we may possess an understanding of the world in which we live is a basic human motivator. Often, the satisfaction of the cognitive needs enable the satisfaction of the basic needs to take place and, in fact, the two are often mutually dependent on each other.

The three primary social motives

These are based upon the work of David McClelland and are:

- the need for achievement (n.Ach.)
- the need for affiliation (n.Aff.)
- the need for influence (n.Inf.) or power (n.Pow.)

The need for achievement

This is the need for measurable personal accomplishment. People high in this need seek out challenging or competitive situations and establish realistic and achievable goals. The concerns of a person with a high n.Ach. are as follows:

1 **Outperforming someone else**. The individual's primary concern is to engage in an activity in which they can win or do better than others. For example, winning a race, doing a better job.
2 **Meeting or surpassing a self-imposed standard of excellence**. Often this self-imposed standard of excellence does not involve

competition with others, but is a self-imposed standard of high-quality performance, e.g. doing an excellent job, finding a better method. The emphasis is not so much on quantity or output, but on working hard to achieve excellence.

3 **Striving to make a unique contribution.** The individual is concerned with having an extraordinary rather than an ordinary accomplishment and in utilizing unique or innovative methods to achieve success.

4 **Setting long-term goals.** This involves the setting of goals beyond the immediate future, often up to 5–10 years ahead.

The need for affiliation

This is the need for being with someone else and/or enjoying mutual friendship. The concerns of a person with a high n.Aff. are as follows:

1 **Being part of a group or team.** The individual enjoys being on the team, sacrifices his or her own needs for the good of the team and enjoys the relationships and companionship that group activities can bring.

2 **Being liked and accepted.** The individual wants to establish, restore or maintain a close, warm and friendly relationship with others.

3 **Maintaining positive interpersonal relationships.** The individual expresses an emotional concern about separation from another person and indicates a desire to restore a close relationship that has previously existed.

4 **Being involved with people in the work situation.** The individual talks about people and working with people as the main focus of his or her occupational life.

5 **Minimizing conflict.** The individual takes steps to avoid conflict and will attempt to establish harmonious interpersonal relationships. This may involve restoring harmony to different relationships.

The need for affiliation (n.Aff) is about the concern of establishing, maintaining or restoring a positive, emotional relationship with another person. The relationship is most adequately described by the word 'friendship'.

Certain interpersonal relationships by themselves are not indicative of n.Aff. For example, mother–daughter, father–son, husband–wife, etc., are all descriptions of a relationship between two people, but they do *not* necessarily mean that the participants in the relationship have a high n.Aff. or indeed that the relationship has the warm companion quality indicated in the definition of n.Aff. These relationships must be further characterized by a concern about maintaining or restoring a positive relationship.

The need for influence or power

This is the need of the individual in attaining an 'influence goal'. The concerns of a person with a high n.Inf. (or n.Pow.) are as follows:

1 **Acquiring a reputation or position**. The individual is concerned with public evaluation. The concern is for positions of high status, to influence the cause of events, and about his or her reputation and the judgement of others of his or her powerful position.
2 **Having control of situations**. The individual is concerned with controlling people and situations. He or she will seek positions or situations where this control can be attained and exercised.

Sometimes the individual will attempt to influence or manipulate by strong or forceful actions such as verbal attacks or by giving support or advice that has not been requested. Such actions may be an attempt to control another person by regulating their behaviour or the conditions of their life.

Analysis of the models

The two models outlined focus on the individual *needs* of the learner. Below are listed a series of needs from the two models. List at least one thing the trainer can do to meet that need in the participant so that he or she has a positive effect on the learning process.

1 Achievement
2 Affiliation
3 Influence
4 Physiological
5 Security
6 Self-esteem
7 Self-fulfilment
8 Self-directedness

Some answers are suggested below.

1 **Achievement**

(a) We set tasks that are neither too easy nor too difficult so that the learners feel a sense of achievement. 'Step-by-step' or 'bite-sized chunks' is the order of the day.
(b) We recognize their achievement by giving positive feedback. While we recognize our own achievements, achievements that go unrecognized by others over a period of time have a demotivating effect.

2 **Affiliation**. We make the individual feel at home by being part of the group, i.e. we reduce any feelings of isolation. We allow ample opportunities for interaction to take place between group members, both during the course and in socializing during out-of-course hours.
3 **Influence**. We give ample opportunities for participation. Syndicate work, individual presentations, co-counselling, all give individuals with a power need the opportunity to assert themselves.
4 **Physiological**. We ensure that the learning environment is appropriate—right temperature, right amount of light, low levels of noise. If the course is residential then facilities are good, particularly

the food! If there are feelings of discontent about this, then delegates cannot focus their minds fully on learning.

5 **Security**. We strive to make individuals feel at ease by reducing tension and anxiety. They must never feel threatened or exposed. Therefore we encourage group interaction and counsel individuals, if appropriate, to create an informal, relaxed, but purposeful atmosphere.

6 **Self-esteem**. We make people feel good about themselves. We give them tasks that are stretching, but ones in which they have a good chance of success. We praise and recognize their accomplishments. We give feedback. We never 'put them down' or destructively criticize. If criticism is needed we allow them to recognize the flaw themselves so that they accept the criticism and will probably commit themselves to improvement. Process reviews using CCTV are a good way of achieving this.

7 **Self-fulfilment**. We give them the opportunity to set their own goals. We support them in an appropriate way to achieve those goals.

8 **Self-directedness**. We give them the opportunity of setting their own learning objectives and, where appropriate, choices in the way in which they learn.

Drive and performance

Most people are goal-orientated. They strive to achieve. Thus the role of the trainer is to harness the drive that this need activates, and not to turn it off.

We must therefore ask the question 'Is there a connection between the amount of drive present and the behaviour that it generates?' Is it merely a question of increasing the drive, in order to increase the performance? Or is there a level at which performance tails off, beyond which an increase in drive will have no positive effect? And what are the differences between individual learners and their capacity to deal with stressful situations?

These are not easy questions to answer. Experiments with rats in 1908 by Yerkes and Dodson indicated a relationship between the level of motivation or arousal and the difficulty of the task. This is shown in Figure 5.2.

If the level of arousal is nil, then the performance is nil. As arousal increases, so does performance, but only to a certain point; beyond this the performance drops. The theory suggests that we all have an optimum level of arousal that produces an optimum performance. As we reach a state of high arousal—anxiety, stress, even fear—then our performance drops. Anyone who has taken a driving test will remember that, while highly motivated, their levels of anxiety may have produced a below par performance (point X on Figure 5.2).

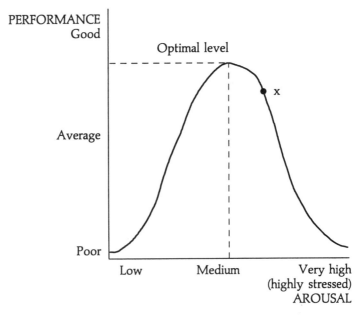

Figure 5.2 *The Yerkes-Dodson law*

It follows, therefore, that there may be a relationship between the difficulty of the task and the level of arousal which, in turn, affects performance. A simple task requires little arousal, so performance is low. At the other end of the spectrum a performance requiring a quantum leap which is beyond the capability of the individual induces no motivation and no performance. Who is motivated to achieve when they know they cannot possibly do it?

The implications of this model for the trainer are:

- tasks must be set which are neither too simple or too difficult, as both lead to reduced motivation, for different reasons.
- the climate or atmosphere in the training room must be neither too stressful or too laid-back. The trainer's own anxiety level (too high or too low) will contribute significantly to this level, as we often project our anxieties and attitudes onto others.

Learning styles

In the previous chapter the experiential learning theory developed by Kolb was outlined. Kolb developed beyond his theory, arguing 'as a result of our hereditary equipment, our particular past life experience and the demands of our present environment, most people develop learning styles that emphasize some learning abilities over others'. He then developed a Learning Style Inventory in order to measure an individual's relative emphasis on each of the four learning abilities. In his view there were four basic styles which he labelled *converger*, *diverger*, *assimilator* and *accommodator*.

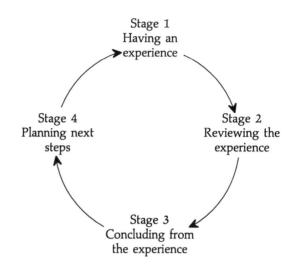

Figure 5.3 *The Honey/Mumford Learning Cycle*

The Learning Style Inventory attracted much criticism and was followed in 1982 by the Learning Styles Questionnaire (Honey and Mumford). This was designed to help individuals discover their preferred learning style(s) so that they could select learning experiences most suitable to their style of learning.

As with Kolb, the LSQ was linked to a four-stage cycle of learning from experience (see Figure 5.3). The four learning styles relate to the four stages in the cycle as follows:

A preference for the *Activist* style—equips you for Stage 1.
A preference for the *Reflector* style—equips you for Stage 2.
A preference for the *Theorist* style—equips you for Stage 3.
A preference for the *Pragmatist* style—equips you for Stage 4.

The four styles, with a brief behavioural description, are as follows:

1 **Activists**. They learn best from activities where they encounter new experiences/problems/opportunities. They enjoy the here-and-now and often thrive in short-term crisis situations. Change, a fast pace and a range of diverse activities to tackle, provide an essential stimulus.

They are usually extrovert individuals who enjoy a high profile position and the stimulus of challenge. Being thrown in at the deep end with a difficult task will be viewed as a challenge not a daunting or overwhelming hurdle. They love to 'have a go'. Routine and longer term consolidation have little appeal.

2 **Reflectors**. The preference here is for a more 'back seat' role. Reflectors like to stand back on the edge of activity and observe what is going on from different perspectives. They are usually good

at data collection and will make a thorough analysis in their own time before coming to conclusions. They like to consider the situation from all angles before acting and so usually they are cautious. Pressure and tight deadlines are not welcomed.

3 **Theorists**. They like concepts, models, theory, systems and the opportunity to explore interrelationships and associations. They like to be stretched intellectually and as they prize logic and rationality, they tend to have analytical minds. Such an analytical preference may mean that they prefer to work on the edge of things, i.e. from a detached position, rather than be involved from within the situation.

4 **Pragmatists**. A preference here indicates an orientation towards relevance between subject matter and one's own position. 'If it works it's good' is the motto, and they look for the earliest opportunity to implement what has been offered. They are practical, down to earth individuals who enjoy problem-solving and making practical decisions. The focus is very strongly on implementation and output.

Learners who score high on all four styles are best equipped to deal with all stages of the learning cycle, but the majority of people will display distinct preferences, with undeveloped styles. The development of these undeveloped styles can form a very useful self-development exercise. There are many advantages in broadening your range of learning skills. As an individual, you can learn much more from everyday experience, while as a trainer you are likely to appeal to and help a wider range of delegates and, therefore, become a more effective trainer.

If significant individual differences in learning styles exist then there are some essential implications for the trainer.

1 It can be used in a training situation to give an individual feedback on their preferences and assist them in planning their own learning opportunities. It may also help them to increase their range of learning.
2 It can give an objective input into the construction of learning groups.
3 It can enable us to refine and improve our understanding of learning skills.
4 It can give trainers objective information about the composition of a group so that they can tailor the methods used to suit the learning styles of the participants.

Exercises

Remember that there is an exercise on page 71 relating to individual needs and two theories of motivation.

1 Obtain a copy of the Learning Styles Questionnaire. Complete it and consider your feedback.

(a) What are your learning strengths?
(b) What styles do you need to develop?
(c) Draw up your own action plan to develop your ability to learn.

2 Consider the learning methods best suited to a group of:

(a) Activists
(b) Reflectors
(c) Theorists
(d) Pragmatists

3 How would you best design a course and choose the methods best suited to a group composed of members with a variety of preferred learning styles?

Summary

Some of the major points from this chapter are as follows:

- Adult students have a wide range of expectations, many of which result from the conditioning process in their formative years.
- Adults have a wide variety of needs which, if harnessed, provide strong motivation for learning. An understanding and recognition of the needs by the trainer can accelerate the learning process.
- From the training standpoint, motivational theory and adult learning theory are closely related.
- Recognition of different styles of learning can help plan courses and assist individual development.

Further reading

C. P. Alderfer, *Existence, Relatedness and Growth*. Free Press, New York, 1972.

F. Hertzberg, *Work and the Nature of Man*. World Publishing Co., Cleveland, Ohio, 1966.

P. Honey and A. Mumford, *A Manual of Learning Styles*. Peter Honey, Maidenhead, 1982.

P. Honey and A. Mumford, *Using Your Learning Styles* (2nd edn). Peter Honey, Maidenhead, 1986.

D. Kolb and R. Fry, 'Towards an applied theory of experiential learning', in *Theories of Group Process* (C. L. Cooper, ed.). Wiley, New York, 1975.

A. H. Maslow, *Motivation and Personality* (2nd edn). Harper & Row, New York, 1954.

D. McClelland, J. W. Atkinson, R. A. Clarke and F. A. Lowell, *The Achievement Motive*. Irvington Publishers, New York, 1976.

D. C. McGregor, *The Human Side of Enterprise*. McGraw-Hill, New York, 1960.

V. H. Vroom, *Work and Motivation*. Wiley, New York, 1964.

R. M. Yerkes and J. D. Dodson, 'The relation of strength of stimulus to rapidity of habit formation', *J. Comp. Neurol. Psychol.* **18** (1908), 459–82.

6 Learning methods

The object of any training event is involvement. The greater the involvement of the learners in the learning process, the greater the learning.

At the end of this chapter you will be able to:

- list a range of participative learning methods;
- select the most appropriate method to increase learning;
- state areas for use of psychometric instruments and identify steps in giving feedback.

Many years ago a group was shocked when they realized that there is not always a direct connection between teaching and learning. Just because someone is teaching there is no guarantee that learning is taking place.

Nevertheless, the prime objective of any teaching session is to help participants learn, and to achieve this objective it is necessary to adopt the appropriate method. Numerous factors can impact upon the choice and these include:

1 The nature of the information or skill to be learned
2 The size of the group
3 Your own strengths or preferences as tutor
4 Resources available, including time.

Item (3) is not as selfish as it first appears. If you choose a method you are uncomfortable with then you will probably give a below-par performance with negative impact on the learning of your delegates.

In choosing a learning method it would be appropriate to remind ourselves of some of the principles of learning outlined earlier.

1 Your students' readiness to learn. Students learn best when they feel a need for the material presented.
2 You must provide an opportunity for your students to *practise* the information or skill you present. The more they work with the material, the better they can do it (*reinforcement*).
3 Provide the opportunity or explore ways in which they can *use* the information or skill you present. Individuals learn best when they can

experience success with the material. This increases both self-confidence and motivation.

There is a wide variety of learning methods available to help your participants learn. Unfortunately, no one method or combination of methods can be applied with equal success in all circumstances. You will have to experiment with several different approaches to find the right one for a particular session.

One very good way is to watch someone else do it. In all walks of life we are always looking for new and better ways of doing things, and training is no exception. Identification with, and imitation of, a fellow professional—particularly a very experienced one—is a powerful way of learning and increasing your own professional competence.

You will also have to develop the ability to decide whether you present information to the whole group or to small sub-groups. Presenting information to a large group is useful because you can:

- give the same information to everyone at one time;
- provide for group interaction;
- help individuals work cooperatively towards a common goal;
- save time.

Presenting information to a small group is time-consuming but you can:

- be more aware of individual needs and be more specific in meeting those needs;
- be more aware of individuals' understanding of your material and any learning difficulties they are experiencing;
- more easily pace your presentation to an individual's learning speed.

Often you will give information to a whole group and then work with individuals or small groups to reinforce your material. Sometimes you can use individual group members to facilitate small group work. Peer facilitation can be a very powerful learning aid as well as a very easy way of coping with large tutor : student ratios.

The range of learning methods

Lecture One of the earliest thoughts of many people who consider a career in the training field is that they have to become lecturers. They feel they must strive to become inspirational orators in front of an audience, and if they cannot then they will not be successful. This is undoubtedly due to tradition and their experience of higher education where the lecture was the predominant mode of instruction.

Many students, as a result of their earlier educational experiences, also expect it and feel most comfortable with it—it is familiar, it is easy to 'hide' in a passive audience and one rarely is challenged or has to confront difficult issues.

Consequently, the lecture is probably the most widely used method in training, although in recent years, with the increasing emphasis on participative methods, its importance has been reduced. Like all the other teaching methods it is extremely effective when used at the right time and delivered in the appropriate way.

Lectures have the following disadvantages:

1 They proceed at one pace and that pace is determined by the lecturer. This is unlikely to suit everyone in the audience.
2 As the interaction is 'one-way', feedback is difficult.
3 They are a strain on the weak, short-term memory capacities of adults (see Figure 6.1).
4 They require a special kind of self-confidence. 'All eyes are on you' and the longer the lecture continues the more your mannerisms, voice, etc., will be scrutinized and critically appraised, often to the detriment of your message.

Despite these disadvantages, when do we use the lecture? As a general 'rule of thumb' we use it when we have to give a mass of information to a large group, and this will be the most economical use of time. Such appropriate times could be when we are:

● developing a background for the course in the opening session;
● presenting material to introduce a topic;
● presenting material supplementary to assignments.

How can we ensure that we become competent lecturers?

1 Strive for the highest degree of informality that can be achieved without losing the respect of the delegates.
2 Stand up when talking and occasionally move back and forth in front of the group.
3 Be aware of the attention span of the audience (see Figure 6.1). Psychologists tell us that during a 30-minute presentation the attention curve steadily drops from an early high to a low after 20 minutes before returning to the early high (presumably when the lecturer indicates the end is near). This has the following implications for the lecturer:

    (a) Keep your presentation short—15 to 20 minutes is probably as much as most adults can absorb.
    (b) Change the pitch, tempo and volume of your voice when speaking.
    (c) Try every device you can think of to add variety, spice and surprise to your presentation.
    (d) Make the key points either very early or very late.

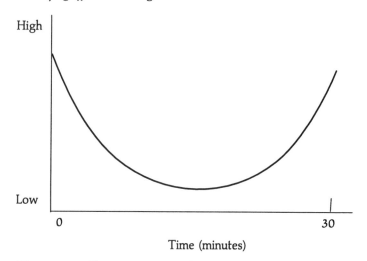

High

Low

0   30

Time (minutes)

Figure 6.1 *The attention span of a group*

4 Eliminate distracting habits and mannerisms and always maintain eye contact with a cross-section of the audience.
5 Have a clearly defined beginning, middle and end. This helps you in the delivery and it also helps your students.

To sum up, the lecture has a very important part to play in imparting information to a lot of people quickly. In terms of structure, 'Tell 'em what you are going to say; tell 'em, then tell 'em what you have told them.' It is best used in short bursts with frequent recourse to alternative, participative methods.

Demonstration Often the best way to get your point across is to actually show or demonstrate what you mean. This can be done by a demonstration *per se* or as a reinforcement or follow-up to a lecture. The way in which one tackles it may depend on the complexity of the operations or principles. Generally, the greater the level of complexity the more you will have to build the demonstration *into* the lecture so that students can actually watch as you demonstrate. This requires extensive use of actual items or visual aids.

The demonstration method is useful because it:

- attracts and holds individuals' attention;
- is easily understood;
- is convincing—it is 'here and now' and imitation is a powerful way of learning;
- ties theory and practice.

The drawbacks of demonstration are:

- Things can go wrong. But by ensuring that you are competent at the task and have prepared thoroughly, then you increase the chance that it will be 'all right on the night'.

- It is often difficult to ensure that everyone can see what you are doing.
- Everyone has to be present. This problem could be overcome if you make a video tape of your demonstration with appropriate close-ups. This ensures that you can reinforce whenever you want as well as overcome the problems of absent members or those unable to see.

During the demonstration you should:

- describe your objectives and procedures clearly;
- show each step slowly and carefully, relating past experiences to future steps;
- check on your effectiveness and the students' understanding by asking questions;
- encourage participants to ask questions;
- supplement with literature, models or other visual aids;
- summarize key points;
- show other applications of the skills or process just presented.

Follow up each demonstration:

- Give participants the opportunity to practise the skills or process just demonstrated.
- Give individual/group help during practice sessions. Often you can use more competent members of the group if your own resources are stretched.
- Raise questions to clarify points.
- Praise and recognize success—a great motivator and confidence builder!
- Help individuals recognize the application of what has been learned to their real-life situations, i.e. facilitate the transfer of learning.

In any training where the emphasis is on *skills* you will use the demonstration method frequently. In terms of the structure, tell them what you are going to do, tell them how to do it, let them practise, and tell them and praise them when they can do it.

Discussion The discussion method is an excellent means of covering the essential points of a session and meeting objectives while allowing individuals to ask questions, raise issues, etc., with everyone else in the group. Sometimes it can be woven into the lecture, in which case the trainer can go beyond the previously recommended 20–30 minutes.

When leading a discussion you should ask questions which serve to provide a general exchange of ideas or facts. It is also a good way of drawing out conflicting opinions. Usually you will find that most adults are willing and anxious to contribute their opinions, even to the point of disagreeing with the leader. This results in interesting and lively discussions which are bound to make more lasting impressions than merely lecturing and giving out facts.

When using the discussion method keep it under control and on the subject—and guillotine it at the right time. In other words, you must ensure that pertinent matters are emphasized and that the time is not monopolized by any particular topic or individual. Too often the discussion degenerates into a 'free for all'. To manage a discussion successfully the leader needs an astute sensitivity to the group and its dynamics, which involves very different skills and approaches from those required for lecturing and demonstrating.

Active, participatory methods

Four main methods will be discussed here:

1 Case study
2 Role play
3 Simulation
4 Games

While these are distinctive methods in their own right there is some overlap. They are all participatory methods with the objective of enabling participants to learn general principles through involvement in a situation as similar to real life as possible. They tend to be used most widely in the field of management training and development and involve a much higher degree of risk for everyone. Often CCTV can be used for giving in-depth feedback and assisting the coaching.

Case study

With this method you present the specific details of a problem, usually in written form, and ask the participants to suggest the best solution they can, based upon the given facts. They must also be prepared to discuss not only their proposal but *why* they reached their decision and, sometimes, *how* they reached their decision. Interesting and varied solutions usually emerge and if several groups tackle the same problem, interesting comparisons can be made which can be shared in a plenary session.

The case study requires:

● lengthy preparation time and may need a couple of 'dry runs' to 'fine-tune' (but be prepared for the comment that there is never enough information!);
● that the facilitator is familiar with the material which should not be a problem if he or she developed it;
● clear and concise briefing to participants;
● debriefing and summarizing skills so that the main points are shared with everyone.

Role play, simulation and games

These may be used to bring together knowledge and experience and to show their interrelationship. They are used widely in skills training— for example, in interviewing, conducting meetings and customer care. Group members are assigned certain roles and are required to work through a problem or situation by acting it out while in character. Sometimes the information used is in the form of a case study.

Role play will become a simulation if it is carried out continuously and intensively over a longer period of time using elaborate materials, with fresh problems and complications introduced periodically.

In management training, business simulations may take place over days rather than hours, with management teams receiving feedback on their decisions and progress from computers.

Sometimes these teams are in competition with others and the exercise could be termed a game.

The advantages of simulations are that they:

- are an enjoyable way to learn if they are realistic;
- require active involvement from participants;
- bring academic subjects alive so that the gap between theory and practice is bridged;
- give participants the opportunity to experiment in 'low risk' situations, where there is no fear of retribution and where as much can be learned from mistakes as from successes;
- are very adaptable to groups of mixed ability, and distinctions between bright and less bright become blurred;
- make it difficult for participants to remain aloof and uninvolved as the enthusiasm of group members is contagious and levels of motivation rise;
- encourage peer facilitation and support because the most able can support the least able;
- increase awareness of participants' own behaviour and the effect on others;
- improve interpersonal skills, team skills and the ability to process information to solve problems and to confront and handle conflict.

Some disadvantages are:

- Role play can degenerate into horseplay, with individuals exaggerating their perception of their role. A firm hand may be required to remind the group of the objective(s) or to bring the role play to a halt. Once this method gets out of hand, you will find it difficult to get a group ever to take it seriously again.
- Lengthy preparation and several 'dry runs' are required.
- It can be very expensive, either because of preparation time or hiring/purchasing charges. Some of the more elaborate business simulations can cost several thousand pounds.
- It involves a high degree of risk. Once the exercise is under way it will not proceed in an orderly, predictable way. The role of the facilitator becomes that of a coordinator. Some may feel very uncomfortable with the loss of control.
- Participants may invest high levels of energy and emotion in the process, which can get out of hand. A high level of sensibility is required and external interventions may be needed.

- Sophisticated equipment may not function predictably so that credibility suffers.
- It requires a lengthy debrief or process review which can make exhausting demands on time and facilitator skills.
- It needs clear and concise briefing for participants, which may require long periods of time.
- Where teams of tutors are required to run elaborate simulations, clashes of philosophy and style can occur.

Open learning   Sometimes called distance learning, this form of learning has enjoyed successful and spectacular growth over the last 20 years. Institutions such as the Open University, the National Extension College and, more recently, the Open Tech Unit of the Training Commission (formerly the Manpower Services Commission), have all made significant contributions to open learning.

There is no universally agreed definition of open learning. It is based on the belief that it is a way of opening up new opportunities for people to learn at a distance from the providing organization.

It usually involves the use of specially prepared self-instructional materials (packages). These are often expensive to produce and buy. These packages are in modular form and each module can be studied on its own or as part of a sequence when they then form a complete course. Learners work through the modules on a step-by-step basis, and study or completion time can vary from a few hours for a single module to months for a complete course.

Open learning packages may utilize a variety of teaching media—from printed material, through audio and video material, to practical work and computer-based training (CBT). Learners usually work through the package on their own but they may meet together with other learners from time to time plus having access to occasional tutorial or counselling support.

Open learning is one answer; it is not the complete answer to many individual and organizational training needs. Its main advantages are as follows:

- It is very flexible in how it can be used. 'Anytime, anywhere' often applies.
- Organizations with few or no training resources can 'plug into it' to develop their people.
- Little time off work is required, which has a particularly strong appeal to the small businessman.
- It meets the self-directed needs of the adult learner.
- The modular structure aids the assimilation process as students progress at their own pace and there is opportunity for reinforcement.
- It is less threatening because there is no group exposure. This can

have a strong appeal to those whose lack of formal education has undermined self-confidence.

There have been many impressive achievements through open learning by those with little formal education, often of mature years, which has resulted in improved self-confidence and job competence. The relatively low cost of tutorial support can make it a cheaper alternative to other forms of learning.

Some of the major disadvantages of open learning are:

- Some of the packages, especially in the field of CBT and Interactive Video, are extremely expensive. Cost-benefit analysis is required before investment is made.
- Good time management skills and study habits are required which many students may not possess, especially if they have had little experience of study.
- The learner is isolated. Many open learners suffer from a lack of support, so that lack of recognition can have adverse motivational effects. Consequently, some programmes experience a high drop-out rate. This is an important hidden cost consideration—a course that is initially cheaper than a traditional course because of absence of tutorial support, is more expensive if there is no completion or end-product. Potential open learners should check on the support available—from the institution, their organization and their family—before committing themselves.
- The lack of group involvement ensures little or no peer support or group identity. It also means that one rich resource for learning—namely, the experience of the adult learner—is rarely used. Opportunities to share, compare and advise with peers are limited.

Open learning can be a useful addition to a company's overall training strategy. It can never replace the traditional group approach but for some subject areas it may be an appropriate and cost-effective way of meeting individual and organizational needs.

Using 'IT' in training Information technology has mushroomed spectacularly in recent years, with an enormous impact upon our lives at work and at home. Inevitably it has impacted upon the training field, in some cases for the better and in others with detrimental results. As with all training aids, IT aids can be a help or a hazard—their success largely depends upon how they are used and managed. This is no different from dealing with people and therefore rather than discuss in detail different forms of IT and how to train with them, I propose to list briefly some of the major principles that should be borne in mind with regard to training with new technology.

Among the types of IT that may be of use are the following:

- Word processors

- Desk-top publishing
- Computer-based training (CBT) and various refinements of CBT
- Viewdata
- Interactive video

People need to be trained in their use and their successful operation should ensure the production of high quality training materials.

Three key points for the trainer to be aware of when using IT are:

- Most trainees working with new technology have little interest in the technology itself. They are not interested in technical specifications or how it works. Their chief interest is 'What will it do for me?'. Once they are sold on the benefits, they are only interested in how to use it and how quickly can they acquire the required skills. The focus on the benefits, therefore, needs to be firmly on the applications of the technology for the job.
- Most trainees are frightened of new technologies. They see IT as threatening and an assault on the status quo. This will be less so with younger trainees, who have recently emerged from an education system in which access to various forms of IT was an everyday event.
- The technology is a means to an end and is not an end in itself or the justification for the learner's attendance.

I once attended a management meeting in which those present were urged to follow a course of action so 'we can help the computer'. Mistaken priorities, perhaps—I had always believed the computer existed to help the trainees!

Some tips for the trainer in terms of method:

- Make instructions simple. How many instruction books and manuals have you read that were written for the expert rather than the novice? Technical jargon clouds understanding and produces alienation and turn-off.
- Make initial tasks simple ('user friendly') to overcome the 'technology resistance' barrier.
- Build simple tasks sequentially, i.e. 'chunk them'.
- Don't patronize the learner, particularly the older one.
- Provide plenty of support, especially in the early stages of tuition. Remember that this can be easily managed if you use the more able members of the group.
- Give regular feedback on performance. This should be built into the programme and also come from the trainer and assistants.
- Let trainees progress at their own rate. Let *them* force the pace—not you or the programme.
- Make everything as interactive as possible.
- Make training with the new technology a fun experience. A half day spent watching youngsters using IT in junior schools may be a very worthwhile experience.

Note: Readers are strongly advised to read Chapter 4, Learning theory, to discover the justification for some of these tips, particularly the sections: A process model of adult learning, Experiential learning, and Memory.

Conclusion The ability to choose the right method for the job is the work of the professional and is part of the set of skills you must develop as you become a competent trainer.

Research indicates that your learners retain about:

10 per cent of what they read;
20 per cent of what they hear;
30 per cent of what they see;
50 per cent of what they both hear and use;
70 per cent of what they say;
90 per cent of what they say and do.

This is shown diagrammatically in Figure 6.2. Though these percentages are only approximations they do indicate that:

● participants learn faster by seeing and hearing than by hearing alone;
● participants learn even faster when doing is added to seeing and hearing;

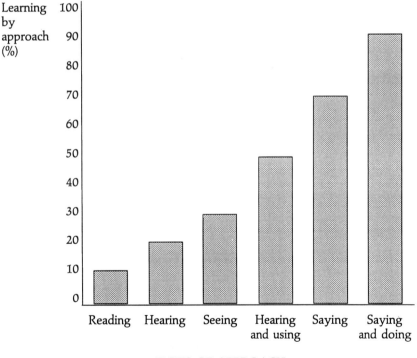

TYPES OF APPROACH

Figure 6.2 *Learning approaches and relative information retention*

- participants retain more of the things they do than of the things they are told.

This breakdown reinforces the effectiveness of some of the more recent developments in learning theories, such as experiential learning theory and accelerated learning outlined in Chapter 4.

By carefully considering your objectives and the nature of the material you plan to cover, you can select the most effective technique or combination of techniques for each session. In the last analysis it is your decision. Some techniques can be used in many different situations; others are only appropriate occasionally. The more methods you have in your repertoire, the easier it will be for you to meet your objectives and the more likely it will be that you will do a better job. Widening your repertoire is a lengthy process, involves risk-taking and is part of your personal development in achieving training competence. Good luck on your journey.

Psychometric instruments

Increasingly in recent years psychometric instruments have been used on management development programmes. This section will focus on their use in training and development, rather than in other areas of application such as selection and succession planning.

The main areas of use for psychometric instruments are:

1 as a tool for self-awareness to assess relative strengths and weaknesses, and to give feedback on managerial and/or leadership style;
2 as a means of building teams, assessing strengths and weaknesses and building more effective units of complementary personality types;
3 as a way of looking at interpersonal relationships in groups to discover why group processes are undermining the effectiveness of the group.

One advantage of using psychometric instruments is the flexibility they offer in terms of administration and use. They can be completed before a course, or during a session; the results can be fed back to the delegate either on a one-to-one basis or in a group situation; and the feedback from them can be reinforced by a variety of methods, particularly in a residential setting where the mind can focus on learning at an intensive level. More will be said about this last advantage shortly.

Group presentation and feedback

In dealing with the instructions for completion, receipt of completed questionnaires, scoring and giving of feedback, the format can vary. Generally, the more complex the instrument the greater will be the time to ascend the learning curve; also, the greater will be the depth of feedback so that there will be a requirement for the delegate to come to terms with it before rejecting or accepting it.

With a complex instrument, such as some detailed personality inventories available, the following format has been largely successful:

1 Questionnaires and answer sheets are given to participants before the course for completion and return. In addition to going over the test instructions, the following points are emphasized:

   (a) it is a self-report instrument;
   (b) there are no right or wrong answers;
   (c) delegates should always think of answering the question in terms of context—work, home, etc.—and thus should consider the feedback in the context in which they completed the questionnaire.

2 Answer sheets are scored and profiles plotted, and feedback may be written before the group presentation takes place.
3 During the presentation, delegates are asked to rate themselves in terms of the style, type, etc., that is being covered by the talk.
4 Individuals are given feedback from the scored questionnaire.
5 With the group's permission, results are shared and comparisons made between:

   (a) individual types in the group;
   (b) self-ratings that they carried out during the presentation.

   Note: Receipt of such feedback requires an atmosphere of openness and honesty as the individual sometimes has to confront himself or herself. It is usually appropriate for the facilitator to share some personal feedback with the rest of the group.

6 Reinforcement takes place through various methods:

   (a) reading;
   (b) co-counselling interviews with others on the programme, particularly delegates' 'more opposite' type;
   (c) behavioural observation of others during the course, especially during practical tasks;
   (d) behavioural awareness of self, e.g. observing CCTV playback.

Individual feedback Sometimes this has to take place on a one-to-one basis. The feedback should be viewed as developmental, not as a judgement or criticism, and the end goals should be:

1 Ownership of the feedback by the individual
2 A commitment to change, where appropriate
3 Some discussion, however preliminary, of follow-up action as part of the individual's development

The feedback is a participative exercise so that everything that is done should be viewed and felt as helpful. This means that the feedback should be carried out in a relaxed atmosphere, free from tension, and characterized by openness and honesty.

Like any interview, it is important to devote time to establishing a rapport. This could be either a relatively short period of time or a longer period. Experience will tend to suggest when the time to move on has arrived. Having sensed that the point to move on has been reached, the following sequence may be appropriate:

1 Explain the test and say how the feedback will be given. It is often useful to reiterate some of the points made at the time the test was administered.
2 Give the feedback:

   (a) Be authentic (open and straight) and non-evaluative.
   (b) Do not take a 'critical parent' role (see page 118).
   (c) Check for understanding by getting the individual to state back what is being said.
   (d) Allow time for resistance (some ideas may take time to get used to).
   (e) Do not become defensive yourself.

   It is often useful here to use phrases such as:

   'The profile indicates that ...'
   'You have reported on yourself that ...'
   'The indications are that ...'

   not

   'You are ...'
   'One area of weakness is ...'
   'This is a poor score on ...'

3 Work with the positives.
4 Discuss indicated weaknesses or development points:

   (a) explore solutions and/or actions;
   (b) consider benefits;
   (c) explore possible avenues for development;
   (d) obtain (if appropriate) a commitment to change, but remember that responsibility for this should rest with the individual;
   (e) check whether any support, e.g. access to yourself or their boss, is wanted.

Exercises

1 List some of the learning methods you have used yourself.

   (a) Which ones do you consider yourself competent at using? Why?
   (b) Which ones do you consider there is room for improvement? What can you do to improve?

2 List some other trainers you have observed who were competent with various methods.

   (a) Why were they competent?

(b) What can you learn from them?

List some times/events when you can experiment with new methods.

3 For each of the following methods, describe a situation in which you might be involved when it might be appropriate to use it:

(a) Lecture
(b) Demonstration
(c) Discussion
(d) Case study
(e) Role play
(f) Simulation
(g) Games
(h) An open learning package

4 Consider a situation where you have received feedback on yourself from a person about a psychometric test you had taken.

(a) How did you react to the feedback? Why?
(b) How did you feel about the feedback? Why?
(c) Consider how the feedback was given. What were the main learning points from it and how can you incorporate them in your own style of giving feedback?

Summary

Some of the major points from this chapter are as follows:

- There is not always a direct relationship between teaching and learning.
- There is a wide range of learning methods, all with advantages and disadvantages. The role of the trainer is to select the most appropriate method in order to optimize learning.
- Participation increases the chances of optimizing learning.
- Instrumented or psychometric feedback is being increasingly used in human resource development activities. A great deal of skill is required in the feedback sessions if maximum value is to be obtained from such a process.

Further reading

A. I. S. Debenham, *A Training Officers Guide for Discussion Leading* (6th impression). BACIE, London, 1981.

H. Ellington, E. Addinall and F. Percival, *A Handbook of Game Design*. Kogan Page, London, 1982.

J. Fripp, *Learning Through Simulations. A Guide to the Design and Use of Simulations in Business and Education*. McGraw-Hill, Maidenhead, 1993.

J. Gentry (ed.), *A Guide to Business Gaming and Experiential Learning*. Kogan Page, London, 1990.

D. Hawkridge, W. Newton and C. Hall, *Computers in Company Training*. Routledge, London, 1988.

B. Hodgson, *Key Terms and Issues in Open and Distance Learning*. Kogan Page, London, 1993.

K. Jones, *A Sourcebook of Management Simulations*. Kogan Page, London, 1989.

K. Jones, *Imaginative Events. A Sourcebook of Innovative Simulations, Exercises, Puzzles and Games*. Vols 1 and 2. McGraw-Hill, Maidenhead, 1992.

G. P. Ladousse, *Role Play*. Oxford University Press, Oxford, 1987.

Morry van Ments, *The Effective Use of Role Play. A Handbook for Teachers and Trainers* (revised edn). Kogan Page, London, 1989.

Morry Van Ments, *Active Talk. The Effective Use of Discussion in Learning*. Kogan Page, London, 1990.

E. Milroy, *Role Play: A Practical Guide*. Aberdeen University Press, Aberdeen, 1982.

P. Race, *The Open Learning Handbook. Selecting, Designing, and Supporting Open Learning Materials*. Kogan Page, London, 1989.

D. Rowntree, *Exploring Open and Distance Learning*, Kogan Page, London, 1992.

T. Russell, *Effective Feedback Skills*. Kogan Page, London, 1994.

M. E. Shaw, R. J. Corsini, R. Blake and S. Mouton, *Role Playing: A Practical Manual for Group Facilitators*. University Associates, San Diego, California, 1980.

B. Tate, *Open Learning Choices for Managers*. Gower, Aldershot, 1995.

7 Managing the group

People's behaviour is modified when they join a group. An understanding of how groups work can help the trainer to manage the group and increase learning.

At the end of this chapter you will be able to:

- list some of the main characteristics of groups;
- list the main stages of group development;
- identify types of behaviour in groups;
- identify a number of roles present within a group and know some techniques of dealing with difficult group members;
- identify some of the differences between training and facilitation;
- list some of the major skills of good facilitation;
- identify some of the different styles of facilitation and their relationship to the different stages of group development.

Characteristics of groups

We spend most of our lives in groups—the family, the class, the sports club, the work group are all everyday examples. The behaviour of individuals is always affected when they find themselves a member of a group and the relationship with different groups of people will often vary considerably. Indeed, the behaviour of individuals can change dramatically when they are in a group.

A group develops a life of its own with established conventions as to what constitutes acceptable behaviour. Within a group individuals may occupy defined positions (roles) such as 'joker', 'militant', etc., and any challenge to established positions or expectations may be strongly resented.

Furthermore, individuals who form part of a group, but break the group's 'rules', are often made to conform again by a variety of means, e.g. gentle persuasion, argument, 'sending to Coventry', etc. Failure to conform can result in expulsion or in the individual deciding to withdraw.

The individuals who constitute a group gradually develop shared ideas and beliefs about what the group is doing and should be doing. These ideas and beliefs, which influence individual behaviour, are termed *norms*. For example, a group at work may develop a low-output norm and any individual who works counter to this will be pressurized to conform or face expulsion—or at least lose much of the social reinforcement the group provides.

People join groups for a variety of reasons, but two generally predominate:

1 To accomplish a task. This is becoming increasingly necessary as most tasks now require an ever-increasing range of specialized skills which are fused together in multi-disciplinary teams.
2 To satisfy the basic needs of the individual member, e.g. the needs outlined in Maslow's hierarchy. Such basic needs were usually first catered for by the family unit.

The mere existence of a group does not ensure that it will operate effectively; a group is effective only to the degree to which it is able to use its individual and collective resources. The measure of the group's effectiveness is its ability to achieve its objectives and satisfy the needs of the individuals within the group.

Sometimes the two functions are compatible with one another; on other occasions they may be incompatible, so that a conflict of interest and priorities for the individual and the group occur.

The extent to which a group can achieve success in its primary role (achieving the task) and its secondary role (social relationships) often depends on how strongly the group is bound together, i.e. its *cohesiveness*. A highly cohesive group will be able to fulfil the task and provide opportunities for social reinforcement, whereas a less cohesive group will have difficulty achieving these goals. Some of the factors affecting group cohesiveness are:

1 **Group size.** Eight to ten people can usually communicate with one another on a face-to-face basis. Beyond this number it becomes more difficult so that sub-groups (cliques) may form who may run counter to the main group.
2 **Status and prestige.** A group that is respected for its efficiency and liked by others will become more cohesive.
3 **Proximity of working** (frequency of contact). The greater the contact, the more opportunity exists for forging a group identity and cohesiveness. Distance brings isolation and problems of inclusion, support, and identity.
4 **Leadership.** The development and cohesion of a group occurs only when there is a feeling of shared leadership among all group members. This means that all group members accept some responsibility for task functions (i.e. those necessary to do the job) and maintenance functions (i.e. those things necessary to keep the group together and interact effectively).

In a training situation there is the complication of leadership identity caused by the role of the tutor/facilitator. Members of the group, and the tutors themselves, bring certain role expectations and a period of mutual adjustment of expectations has to take place, particularly in the early days.

5 **Goals and objectives**. For any group to operate effectively, it must have stated goals and objectives. In addition, the group members must be committed to the goals. Such commitment comes from involving all group members in defining the goals and relating them to specific problems that are relevant to group members. The time spent on goal definition in the early stages of a group's life results in less time needed later to resolve problems and misunderstandings.

In the training situation, it is suggested that the setting of objectives should be a mutual contract between learners and facilitator and that it should be done at the start. That way there is ownership of, and commitment to, the programme objectives.

6 **Group climate**. This is always difficult to define but involves effective interpersonal communication and a high level of energy. Effective interpersonal communication is about group members communicating in an open and honest manner and requires that they listen to one another and attempt to build on each other's contribution.

Energy is contagious and high levels can generate enormous enthusiasm and commitment and have a synergistic effect.

The facilitator has an enormous effect upon group climate, particularly in the early days. If he or she is enthusiastic and committed—and can communicate that to group members—then there is a good chance that a positive climate will be established.

Furthermore, the skill of listening and building on members' contributions is even more important for the facilitator, as he or she has the role of welding the group into an effective unit.

Stages of group development

It has been well documented that groups go through several well-defined stages of development from their first meeting to their eventual disbandment.

Stage 1: 'Ritual sniffing'

This is a newly formed, uncertain group in which the majority of members (facilitator included) are feeling uncertain and anxious. This will probably manifest itself in a variety of defensive behaviours, such as quiet and reserved, or outgoing and loud.

Individuals are going through a process of 'weighing up'. Group members are weighing up the tutor and the rest of the group, and the tutor, both consciously and unconsciously, is weighing up the group. A mental process of establishing oneself in relationship to others is evident. The concern is more with not making a fool of oneself and, therefore, risk-taking is low.

At this stage, the role of the facilitator is to establish credibility and put people at ease. A non-threatening, ice-breaking activity is ideal for starting.

As the group develops there is a gradual increase in individual interaction. This can take place in the classroom or over a coffee break. Friendships and bonds are at a very superficial level and the role of the facilitator is to encourage interaction whenever possible so that deeper, more meaningful, relationships can be formed.

Stage 2: 'Jockeying for position'

At this stage relationships develop. There is usually less tension and anxiety and individuals begin to vie for positions of power and influence. Certain significant individuals who adopt significant roles begin to emerge.

The facilitator's job is to 'tune in' to the dynamics of the group and the emerging roles. The facilitator must continue to earn the respect of the group, otherwise his or her leadership will be threatened or undermined.

During this stage the group begins to decide its *modus operandi*. Important questions that are asked and addressed are:

1 Who controls the group? Will it change from its early, strong dependence on the facilitator?
2 How will control be exercised? Will the more authoritarian style of the facilitator be reduced, and by how much; and how will the group take responsibility for its own destiny?
3 How do we deal with individuals who do not appear to be conforming to the rapidly emerging group norm? This is an important question for the facilitator—and also for the group members.

These questions need to be confronted and answered if the group is to proceed. Many groups fail to find a way of dealing with their control problems and so experience 'process difficulties' which result in a less positive learning experience.

Stage 3: 'Getting the act together'

After resolving the control issues, the group organizes itself. A group identity begins to form, people are committed to the group and each other. They want to achieve success.

At this stage the group assigns tasks, roles are clarified and the members collaborate to support each other and solve problems. A more democratic or coaching style of facilitation is usually more appropriate for the facilitator.

This stage is usually characterized by a high energy level and commitment. Individuals respect each other, the facilitator and their contributions, even if they do not always agree. There is a commitment to conflict resolution. New ways of doing things are explored, the quality of listening improves if for no other reason than the level of security is higher and the level of anxiety is lower.

There is also humour in greater abundance. People can usually laugh at themselves as well as at each other. Defensive barriers have largely been removed.

Stage 4:
Maturity

Group members have forged a strong group identity and have developed rapport and closeness. Sometimes this is so strong that bonds of friendship are forged that may even last a lifetime. Members sometimes form an informal support network long after the group has been disbanded.

The group's workings are characterized by informality, humour and a high level of support for each other. People are not afraid to ask for help if they need it and help is readily given.

At this stage, it is impossible for any outsider to be integrated into the group. Indeed, the danger for a group at this level of development is that it can be so insular as to be unaware of, or unwilling to consider, outside influences that could be beneficial.

The facilitation style should now be much less directive. Sometimes the group can become so self-directing that facilitator contribution is not needed, although there is a danger that this could be perceived as 'abdication of responsibility' by the group. It may be appropriate to renegotiate the relationship with the group, perhaps to become a process consultant to guard against complacency.

Stage 5:
Old age

There is an optimum time for a group to be together to accomplish the task and meet the social needs of its members. Beyond a certain point continuation becomes counter-productive. This stage has been reached when it becomes difficult to introduce novelty, creativity is dropping, and apathy and cynicism are beginning to set in.

If new experiences cannot be introduced or shared, it is usually appropriate to disband the group. The trick really lies in disbanding just before the rot sets in. In the same way that individuals can stay too long in a job, so groups can stay together too long so that the warm feelings and memories are erased by experience of this last stage.

Endings are always difficult. In many ways they are more difficult than making good beginnings. It is important, though, that time and energy are devoted to this process so that members 'look back with affection' rather than 'look back in anger'.

Group behaviour

To analyse a small group at work, while also being a member, is a complex and difficult task. It means not only observing the group and its members but also being acutely aware of how your own behaviour (your attitudes, your physical presence, your body language, your views, etc.) impacts upon others and contributes to the character of your particular group.

The field of group dynamics is complex but intriguing. An understanding of it can greatly enhance one's knowledge of self, others, and the way groups function. A knowledge and understanding of the importance of *process* in group workings can have enormous benefits.

Below is a list of questions that could be used to explore the dynamics of group behaviour. The questions relate to any group and use their experience and development as the primary resources for looking at the subject. This list is by no means exhaustive and can be used in a variety of ways and thus the intention is not to be prescriptive but to use judgement according to the situation.

1 What were your feelings when the group first met: concern; anxiety; doubt; hostility; warmth; others? Why did you feel as you did?
2 Do you feel the same now as you did at the start? If you feel differently:

  (a) In what way do you feel you have changed?
  (b) What has caused the change?

3 How would you describe the atmosphere/climate within the group at this stage of the course? Has it always been the same?
4 What do you consider has been the effect of the course tutor(s) on the group?
   What do you consider has been the effect of the group on the course tutor(s)?
   What do you consider have been the effects of the course tutors on each other?
5 Do you consider that the course tutors have been accepted as members of the group? Alternatively, have they been perceived as being 'above and beyond' the group?
6 Have any members of the group taken on any particular roles?
   What are these roles? What have they contributed to the group?
   Who has been more 'task' orientated?
   Who has been more concerned with the social and emotional problems of the group?
7 Has one person emerged as 'group leader'? Or has the 'leader' varied, according to task and circumstance?
8 Do some members contribute more to discussion than others?
   Are some members reticent and shy?
   How has this been dealt with? Were the group members always

aware of, and sensitive to, the needs and interests of the other group members?

9   Have members learned from each other in the group?

10 Can you identify a specific pattern of development in the group?

11 Have any sub-groups or cliques formed within the group?

12 As the group has developed and hopefully become more cohesive, has its progress affected the attitudes, feelings and contributions of individuals within it?

13 Do you consider the size, age range, sex ratio and background have been appropriate?

14 Can you think of *one word* that describes this group?

15 Have there been any external influences upon this group? If so, what has been the result?

16 How does this group compare with other groups that you have been involved with?
    What are the main differences, and why?

Dealing with difficult members

Whatever the level and whatever the subject, one thing can be guaranteed: you will have a heterogeneous group. To the facilitator is given the impossible task of welding them into an effective unit.

It is often the case that among the motley crew there will exist some difficult members whose behaviour taxes your group facilitation skills and can have a detrimental effect on group development and learning.

Below is a list of some of the stereotypes you could encounter and some ways of handling them.

1 **The positive type**. They are a great help in discussion, particularly when members are not very forthcoming. Use them frequently.

2 **The talkative type**. Intervene tactfully and limit their speaking time.

3 **The shy type**. Try to bring them into the discussion with easy questions. Always give credit wherever possible and increase their self-confidence.

4 **The persistent questioners**. They will try to trap the trainer or discussion leader. Try to deal with questions tactfully and check that you have satisfied their question. *Never* get involved in an argument—it reduces your credibility and the group will take their side.

   If you do not know the answer, *admit it*. Either offer to find out after the class or ask the group if anyone can shed light on the issue.

   If they persist, throw it back to the group—they will usually deal with an aggressive individual most effectively.

5 **The know-all or arrogant type**. Let the group deal with their theories and viewpoints.

6 **The argumentative type**. Stay quiet and do not get involved. The group will deal with the problem themselves. Always try to stop them monopolizing.

7 **The uncooperative type**. Recognize their knowledge and experience and use them wherever possible. Be aware of their needs and play on them.

8 **The thick-skinned uninterested type**. Ask them about their work or interests. They must have some! Try to relate topic matters to that and ask for a contribution. By relating it to where they 'are at' or 'coming from' usually raises interest.

9 **The intellectually superior type**. Listen and consider but do not criticize and do not be provoked. Use the 'yes—but' technique or 'agree to disagree'. Check out what other group members think.

Facilitation

You know that I don't believe that anyone has ever taught anything to anyone. I question the efficiency of teaching. The only thing that I know is that anyone who wants to learn will learn. And maybe a teacher is a facilitator, a person who puts things down and shows people how exciting and wonderful it is and asks them to eat.

(Carl Rogers, 1983)

As our knowledge of the learning process in the adult increases and the importance of adopting an experiential approach gains increasing acceptance, a more participative approach to training has manifested itself. With this participative style, the role of the trainer has changed from that of teacher to that of facilitator.

Facilitation applies to group situations, with the size of the group not usually exceeding 15. In fact, even this number can present group management problems so that a split into sub-groups may be appropriate.

Facilitation is defined by Bentley (1994) as: 'the provision of opportunities, resources, encouragement and support for the group to succeed in achieving its objectives, and to do this through enabling the group to take control and responsibility for the way they proceed.'

Facilitation is one of the key skills of a set adviser with Action Learning Sets (see Chapter 4) which is the area in which the author has had most experience of facilitation. It is the intention, therefore, to use the model of Action Learning to discuss the following:

● The three main areas of facilitation.
● The main styles of facilitation.
● The main skills of facilitation.
● The relationship of styles and skills to the evolving group or set.

Main areas of facilitation

These are as follows:

1 **Subject content**. Any group in a learning or training situation will expect to receive tuition to increase either their knowledge or skill

level. These are two of the three main areas in which we learn (see Chapter 4).

2 **Process**. This refers to the way in which group members decide to learn and deal with their content.

3 **Group management**. Every group is composed of individuals, giving each group its own unique identity. The group needs to decide what encouragement and support it will need, how it will proceed, and what demands it will make on the facilitator. Here, there will be a contracting process between group members and the set adviser which will evolve over a period of time.

In Action Learning, learning is depicted by Revans (1971, 1983) in terms of the following equation:

$$L = P + Q$$

in which

$$
\begin{aligned}
L &= \text{Learning} \\
P &= \text{Programmed knowledge} \\
Q &= \text{Ability to ask the right questions at the right time and to take action}
\end{aligned}
$$

The relationship between P and Q, and also between subject content and process, is shown in Figure 7.1. In the author's experience, this applies equally to Action Learning Sets who are either pursuing a qualification or non-qualification programme.

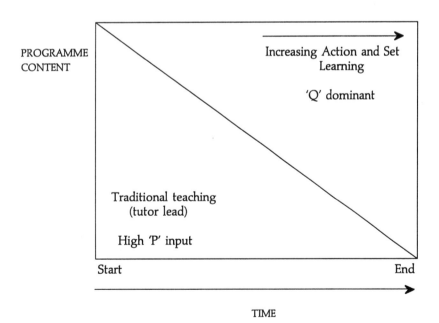

Figure 7.1 *Learning Sets*

As time passes and as the set evolves, the amount of input from the tutor (initially very high) will decrease, perhaps to zero. The set begins to take increasing responsibility for its own learning so that the role of the set adviser changes from subject expert and tutor to that of facilitator, and not only with regard to subject content but also—with increasing importance—to group process and interaction.

At the outset, set members may be confused, and need direction. 'Tell us what to do', 'Tell us what is required', or 'Lead us', they cry. They are passive and initially dependent. To meet these needs and to establish their own credibility, the set adviser should take the lead and should direct and take full responsibility for presenting subject material. As the set develops, hopefully to a mature stage in which it is functioning effectively, the role and skills required of the set adviser change—from a 'hands-on' to a more 'hands-off' approach. These skills and their evolving emphases are listed in Table 7.1.

Table 7.1 *Facilitation and group development*

Stage of group development	Stage 1: 'Ritual sniffing'	Stage 2: 'Jockeying for position'	Stage 3: 'Getting the act together'	Stage 4: Maturity	Stage 5: Old age
Facilitation style	Directive 'Hands on'	Persuasive Influencing	Supportive Letting go	Occasional support 'Hands off'	Empowering for future self-directed learning
Facilitation skill	Content expert Leading Presenting Directing Guiding	Encouraging Challenging Questioning Probing Counselling Giving feedback 'Mirroring back'	Developing/ moving forward Listening—summarizing —reflecting Focusing Coaching Tapping and developing expertise	Delegating Abdicating	Making good endings

TIME

→

NOTE: This table does not seek to suggest that particular skills are required only at a certain stage but seeks to emphasize that, as a group develops, facilitation skills change and evolve, with different emphases.

The objective of the set adviser/facilitator is to wean the group off its dependency so that it takes increasing responsibility for its own learning and its method of working. I would also argue that the set adviser should have two major goals which should have been achieved by the time the set disbands:

● To produce clearly measurable outputs, in the form of work-related projects completed for presentation to the employing organization—

who have the option to implement if appropriate (so giving a return on investment in training).

- To empower set members to believe in themselves and help themselves in the future, and, from this platform of increased self-confidence, to explore and strive to reach their full potential by taking responsibility for their own learning and development.

For the facilitator, like the good parent, the ultimate objective is to hand over responsibility without fuss or trauma. From ancient China, the following quotation is most apt:

A leader is best
When people barely know that he exists,
Not so good when people obey and acclaim him,
Worst when they despise him.
Fail to honour people
They fail to honour you;
But of a good leader, who talks little,
When his work is done, his aim fulfilled,
They will say, 'We did this ourselves'.

(Lao Tzu)

Some of the ways in which the facilitator may manage the group process will now be addressed.

Some skills of facilitation

These can be listed under three major headings each of which correspond to the three main areas of facilitation outlined earlier:

1 **Subject expert**. This is important at the start of the life of the set and to help establish credibility. Therefore, at this stage, skills in presenting are required.

   As the group evolves, this skill should be less to the fore, and the skill changes to one of recognizing other expertise and knowledge in the set, and harnessing it for the benefit of all.

2 **Group manager**. As the group evolves, less direction is required, with the responsibility for direction being handed over to the set. The time required for this change will vary and the facilitator should 'let go' at an appropriate rate, according to the group's readiness to direct itself. At *no* stage should facilitation be equated with either control or manipulation.

   The key skill that emerges relates to intervention—knowing when and how to intervene is only developed through experience. Interventions can take numerous forms, each one of them requiring a skill development, and these include:

   (a) challenging the group or its members about outcomes or its way of working;
   (b) encouraging when the way ahead is unclear;
   (c) 'mirroring back' or summarizing what has been discussed, in an objective and unbiased manner;

(d) giving feedback to individuals and the set, on the way of working or the outcomes, which may include written assignments;

(e) counselling individuals when problems arise;

(f) asking open and probing questions;

(g) coaching individuals and the set;

(h) knowing when to 'let go' but doing so in such a way that the set swims and does not sink.

3 Process consultant. This mainly involves advising and commenting upon how the set operates and deals with its content and findings.

Characteristics of a good facilitator

Some of the main characteristics can be listed as follows:

- Sensitivity to people and situations—this is vitally important if interventions are to be successfully made
- Perception and quickness of mind
- Tolerance of ambiguity
- Patience
- Openness, candour, and trust—this is important if a trusting and open climate is to be established within the set
- Strong desire to see others learn and develop—a good facilitator should rejoice in others' success
- Empathy—being capable of 'operating through the mind of another person'
- Conceptual ability
- High awareness of self
- Recognizes the importance of process as well as content and end product.

Exercises

Reflect on some training events in which you have been involved, either as a trainer, participant or observer.

1 Consider a 'difficult' group.

(a) Why was it 'difficult'?

(b) How was (were) the problem(s) dealt with?

(c) What could have been done differently to improve the outcome?

(d) What are the major learning points from your observations?

2 Consider some 'difficult' individuals.

(a) Why were they 'difficult'?

(b) How were they dealt with?

(c) What (if anything) could have been done differently?

(d) What are the major learning points from your observations?

Summary   Some of the major points from this chapter are:

- Groups are a powerful vehicle for learning.
- Groups usually go through distinct stages of development.
- A knowledge of groups and group behaviour can assist in the management (not control) of groups.
- Groups can often contain difficult members, each requiring different methods of management. Do not underestimate the power of the group in dealing with difficult members.
- Facilitation requires many more skills beyond those employed by the traditional trainer, particularly in the area of group management.
- The aim of facilitation is to encourage and give the group or set increasing responsibility for taking control of its own learning.

Further reading

B. Auvine, B. Densmore, M. Extrom, S. Poole, and M. Shanklin, *A Manual for Group Facilitators*. Centre for Conflict Resolution, Madison, Wisconsin, 1977.

T. Bentley, *Facilitation. Providing Opportunities for Learning*. McGraw-Hill, Maidenhead, 1994.

S. Brookfield, *Understanding and Facilitating Adult Learning: A Comprehensive Guide to Principles and Effective Practices*. Jossey Bass, San Francisco, 1976.

D. Cartwright, 'The nature of group cohesiveness', in *Group Dynamics Research and Theory* (D. Cartwright and A. Zander, eds). Harper & Row, New York, 1968.

T. Douglas, *Groups—Understanding People Gathered Together*. Tavistock Publications, London and New York, 1983.

L. Hart., *Faultless Facilitation*. Kogan Page, London, 1992.

J. Heider, *The Tao of Leadership*. Wildwood House, Aldershot, 1986.

J. Heron, *Facilitator's Handbook*. Kogan Page, London, 1989.

J. Heron, *Group Facilitation: Theories and Models For Practice*. Kogan Page, London, 1993.

G. Houston, *The Red Book of Groups and How to Lead Them Better*. Rochester Foundation, Rochester, 1984.

D. Jacques, *Learning In Groups* (2nd edn). Kogan Page, London, 1991.

J. E. Jones, 'Dealing with disruptive individuals in meetings', in *The 1980 Annual Handbook for Group Facilitators* (J. W. Pfeiffer and J. W. Jones, eds). University Associates, San Diego, California, 1980.

H. Knowles and M. Knowles, *Introduction to Group Dynamics* (2nd edn). Association Press/Follett, Chicago, 1972.

D. Leigh, *A Practical Approach to Group Training*. Kogan Page, London, 1991.

R. W. Revans, *Developing Effective Managers*. Longman, Harlow, 1971.

R. W. Revans, *The Origins and Growth of Action Learning*. Chartwell Bratt, Bromley, 1982.

R. W. Revans, *ABC of Action Learning*, Chartwell Bratt, Bromley, 1983.

M. Robson, *Facilitating*. Gower, Aldershot, 1995.

C. Rogers, *Freedom to Learn*. Merrill, Columbus, Ohio, 1983.

J. Schwab, M. Baldwin, J. Gerber, M. Gomori and V. Satir, *The Satir Approach to Communication: A Workshop Leaders Manual*. Science and Behaviour Books, Palo Alto, California, 1989.

T. Spinks and P. Clements, *A Practical Guide to Facilitation Skills. A Real World Approach*. Kogan Page, London, 1993.

Lao Tzu, *The Way of Life* (trans. Witter Bynner). Perigee Books, New York, 1980.

A. Zander, *Groups at Work*. Jossey Bass, San Francisco, 1977.

8 The communication process in training

To be a competent trainer you must be able to communicate. The better you are at communicating, the more successful you are going to be as a trainer.

At the end of this chapter you will be able to:

- state the main components of the communication system and their relative importance;
- state and be able to use some of the skills of effective verbal and non-verbal communication;
- identify and use some models to improve your ability to communicate.

Interpersonal communication is at the very heart of the training process. The Oxford Dictionary definitions are as follows:

- to communicate (*verb*): impart, transmit, share, receive.
- communication (*noun*): the act of imparting a piece of information given a connection between places.

Success in training is directly related to your ability to communicate. Communication is a two-way process in which information is sent, received and acknowledged, as Figure 8.1 shows.

The model can also be reversed because the receiver, by acknowledging the message, also becomes the sender.

The types of communication that exist in the training situation include

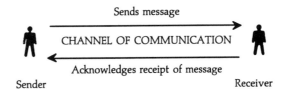

Figure 8.1 *The communication process*

- verbal
- written
- non-verbal (body language)
- visual
- tactile
- aromatic

In order to receive each type of communication we need to be able to:

- listen
- feel
- see
- smell

As Figure 8.1 shows, the parties need to be able to send and acknowledge messages and to change constantly from both positions.

The channel is the means by or through which the message is conveyed between the various parties. Some examples of channels of communication are the telephone (verbal), face (non-verbal), meeting (verbal and visual), a report or handout (written), TV (verbal, visual), aftershave, perfume (aromatic), a specimen (visual, tactile), etc.

Communication is therefore a two-way process. Unfortunately, the channels can become blocked when barriers are erected. The barriers can be:

- physical, e.g. deafness or inability to see the sender;
- emotional, e.g. insecurity, anxiety, feeling threatened or exposed, fear.

As trainers, we must strive to ensure that when barriers occur they are removed and that proper communications exist. We must ensure, sometimes on our own, sometimes with group help, that the physical and emotional barriers are removed.

It is important, therefore, to stress that the competence of a good trainer requires (a) skill not only in giving information (presenting) but in receiving it, and (b) an awareness of barriers to communication and their removal in an appropriate manner.

Verbal communication

You do not have to be a brilliant orator possessed of inspirational qualities to become a competent trainer. Undoubtedly, some are better at communicating than others. The objective of the communication process is clarification, not amplification, and with this objective in mind we should remember KISS—Keep It Short and Simple. Jargon, unless appropriate to the audience, should be eliminated.

Here are a few simple tips to help you improve your verbal communication skills when actually presenting:

- Be relaxed.
- Smile at the audience. It is a wonderful ice-breaker and it shows you are human.
- Maintain good eye contact with the whole audience. Look at them as individuals and do not stare for long spells at any one person.
- Be well-rehearsed. This should aid the flow and reduce 'ers' and 'umms'.
- Be confident.
- Be credible. Establish your credibility early and *never* apologize for your presence.
- Be enthusiastic. Enthusiasm is contagious. If *you* do not believe it, how can you expect your audience to believe it?
- Be appropriately dressed. It gives you confidence, projects a professional image and demonstrates your respect for the audience.
- Be audible:
  - speak up;
  - vary the pitch and avoid monotone;
  - avoid the tendency to speak too quickly.
- Interact with the audience if appropriate. This can be done by asking questions and is easier with smaller groups than large audiences. You can relate to them as individuals and use their knowledge and answers as a reference point, i.e. you start where *they* are at, and make your presentation relevant to *them*—and you immediately build up rapport with them.
- Be clear. Use simple, concise language and avoid jargon wherever possible.
- Use clear, concise terminology, appropriate for the audience. Avoid jargon.
- Use your hands and arms to emphasize points. Do not go over the top with your gesticulations and do not be statuesque. Avoid distracting mannerisms as they can be the focus of attention for the audience.
- Use appropriate humour. A well-received joke can reinforce or lighten the proceedings but a poorly received one can cause embarrassment for presenter and audience. 'Tune-in' to your audience first.
- Remember everyone is nervous before presenting but also remember nervousness is not as obvious to the audience as to the presenter. This should help your confidence. Good preparation and rehearsal should inspire confidence. Remember also that in nearly every case the audience is on your side—they want you to succeed, not to fall flat on your face!
- Vary the pace. Be aware that nerves tend to make us speak more quickly. Try therefore to err on the side of speaking slowly rather than quickly. Vary the pace and remember also the value of silence— a pause is a very effective way of getting your audience's attention.
- Speak for an appropriate length of time. Remember the attention

curve (see Figure 6.1) and do not go on too long.
- Deal with questions by:
  - anticipating beforehand;
  - listening with full concentration;
  - acknowledging the questioner with something like, 'Thank you. I'm glad you raised that';
  - answering as fully as possible.

Do not

- flannel—if you do not know, admit it. Either seek the answer from the group or suggest you will find out and come back to the questioner;
- put a questioner down. However stupid or irrelevant the question, do not be sarcastic or rude;
- argue. Avoid confrontation and, as a last resort, 'agree to disagree'.

Non-verbal communication

The study of non-verbal communication (NVC) or body language is a recent phenomenon and researchers have noted and recorded almost one million non-verbal cues and signals. Mehrabian found that the total impact of a message is

7 per cent verbal (words only)
38 per cent verbal (including tone of voice, etc.)
55 per cent non-verbal.

Birdwhistel estimated that the average person speaks for a total of 10–11 minutes per day and that the average sentence takes only about 2½ seconds. He endorsed the findings of Mehrabian, saying that the verbal component of face-to-face conversation is 35 per cent and that 65 per cent of communication is done non-verbally.

There now appears to be widespread agreement that the verbal channel is used mainly for conveying information and the non-verbal channel conveys interpersonal attitudes and emotions, which may or may not accord with the verbal message. It is amazing, how we are often unaware that the messages our bodies are transmitting tell a very different story from our verbal message.

It is not suggested that, as trainers, we should become experts in the field of NVC. But we must be aware that body language can communicate attitudes to which the group will undoubtedly respond. By being aware of the importance of NVC we can become much better communicators.

Conversely, we must also be aware of the messages that the individuals in the group are sending us, and which may necessitate a change in style, pace, activity, etc.

In short, we must be aware of our own NV messages and of those that the group send to us.

Here are a few tips to help you develop your ability to communicate by increasing your awareness of body language:

DO	DON'T
Have an open posture	Cross your arms
Smile	Frown or scowl
Maintain eye contact	Look away or stare at one person
Look at the person	Point with one finger
Sit forward, if seated	Slouch in a chair, hide behind a
Have a relaxed appearance	desk or place your feet on desks
Have open palms	or tables
Have hands at side	Appear tense and anxious
Arms outspread with open	Clench your fists
palms	Have hands in pockets
Have legs uncrossed	Have hands hidden
	Chew your pencil

Notice the importance of the eyes and the hands. The left-hand column encourages openness, trust and a relaxed, purposeful interaction; the right-hand column encourages defensiveness, mistrust, anxiety and negative interactions.

We actually project our openness or anxieties onto the group who will respond accordingly. One problem of team teaching is that if there is an atmosphere of tension and anxiety between the team, then the group will 'latch on' to it and respond accordingly.

Moral: Whether working on your own or with others, get your own act together first before unleashing yourself on the group.

Personal space or distance

The principle of 'territoriality' has been well established by numerous biological studies of animals. Only recently have we realized that man, too, has spatial needs which can be affected by such factors as culture, status, role, etc.

Research by Allan Pease has indicated that there are four distinct zones that people usually maintain when communicating:

1 **The intimate zone** is 6–18 inches (15–45 cm) from the body, and is the zone that we look upon as our own property. Only those emotionally close to us are permitted to enter it. This includes lovers and close family and friends.
2 **The personal zone** is 18–48 inches (45–120 cm) from the body, and is the distance over which we interact at social events, particularly when we know people well.
3 **The social zone** is 4–12 feet (1.5–3.5 m) from the body and is the distance at which we stand from strangers.

4 **The public zone** has a range of over 12 feet (3.5 m) and is a comfortable distance from which to address a group of people.

The distance that would be acceptable in the training situation would be either the 'social' or the 'public zone'. Among the factors impacting upon the choice would be the physical nature of the room, type of training and nature of the task, and stage of the group development and personality of the learners and trainer(s). In determining distance and layout a good rule of thumb is to choose what you *feel* comfortable with. Your comfort or anxieties will be projected onto the group with a consequent positive or negative impact upon the learning process.

Active listening

In the training situation, as in our working and everyday lives, we tend to believe that the better we are at talking the better we shall be able to communicate. We tend to give little attention to the listening part of the communication process, which is truly amazing when we consider the statistics given in Table 8.1.

Table 8.1 *Forms of communication*

	Listening	Speaking	Reading	Writing
Learned	1st	2nd	3rd	4th
Used	Most (45%)	Next most (30%)	Next least (16%)	Least (9%)
Taught	Least	Next least	Next most	Most

Reproduced from *A Guide to Listening* by Ian MacKay, British Association for Commercial and Industrial Education, 2nd impression, 1990.

On average people with normal learning retain only 25 per cent of what they hear. There are many reasons why this is the case:

1 We perceive listening as a passive activity and find the prolonged concentration required impossible to maintain.
2 The average person speaks at about 130 words per minute, whereas our thinking speed is about 500 words per minute. Consequently, we are continually jumping ahead of what is actually being said. We often, therefore, go on 'mental walkabout', thinking of other things.
3 We don't clear our minds beforehand and so the 'noise in our system' shuts out or distorts what is being said.
4 The listener is tense with emotion so that his or her ability to listen is seriously impaired.
5 We are concerned with our reply so that the concentration is on this rather than what is being said to us.

6 The perception of the listener may so differ from the perception of the talker that a totally different and incorrect interpretation of the information may occur.

All of these factors can ensure that the message received is not the message sent. In some cases it may not even bear the slightest resemblance!

How can we improve our listening? Quite simply by getting the sender of the message (learner) involved with the receiver (trainer). The communication becomes two-way so that the learner is involved in the learning process and the process of addressing and solving problems is improved.

The technique of making the process of communication two-way is called *active listening*, and is an active not a passive process (see Figure 8.3). The steps in active listening are:

1 *A* sends a message.
2 *B* receives the message. This involves concentration and working out the implications of the message.
3 *B* states back what has been understood, but *makes no evaluations*.
4 *A* either agrees with *B*'s interpretation or sends the message again if any misunderstanding has occurred.
5 The process is continually repeated, once understanding by both parties has been achieved.

Two techniques that can help us become more competent at active listening are 'summarizing' and 'reflecting'.

Summarizing This is concerned with the factual side of the message and involves stating back to the speaker the listener's understanding of the information. This paraphrasing should take place at regular intervals and has the advantages of:

- checking understanding;
- offering opportunity for clarification;
- showing the speaker that you have been listening to what has been said, thus demonstrating your interest;
- giving the speaker feedback on how well the message has been expressed.

Useful phrases are:

'As I understand it, what you're saying is ...'
'So your point is that ...'

Reflecting Reflecting deals with the speaker's feelings which may or may not be mentioned overtly. Such recognition of the speaker's feelings builds empathy between you. It enhances your understanding of the situation and of the person and improves the communication process.

Useful phrases are:

> 'That must have made you very annoyed'
> 'You felt that ...?'
> 'That must have been very satisfying for you'.

When reflecting, the listener acts as a mirror of the speaker's feelings, but does not pass comment or evaluate those feelings. Care must also be taken that our non-verbal signals—e.g. tone of voice, facial expression, etc.—do not communicate a judgement of the speaker.

Active listening is most used in the counselling situation, often on a one-to-one basis. It is of benefit in the training situation—e.g. when a learner is experiencing difficulty with the subject matter, when the learner disagrees with what the trainer has said, or in clarifying the content of a question.

Appropriately used, active listening can bring many benefits to the training situation.

- It shows the learners that you want to hear what they have to say. If you show people you are prepared to listen to them, they will be more willing to listen to you.
- It acknowledges the learners' presence and also their experience. Utilizing their experience adds to the richness of learning for the group.
- It encourages a climate of openness and trust, and this improves communication.
- It helps the trainer 'tune in' to individuals in the group and to recognize problems.
- It helps break down learner resistance by getting them more involved in the learning process.
- It recognizes the importance of feelings in the communication process.
- It keeps the responsibility for learning and achieving solutions where it belongs—with the learner.
- It encourages a continuation and improvement in the communication process.

A comparison between active and passive listening is summarized in Figures 8.2 and 8.3.

Transactional Analysis

Transactional Analysis (TA) is based on a theory of personality and communication, and provides a useful model for understanding and improving interpersonal relations and communication. It is a method of analysis to help an individual determine the basis from which another individual is communicating or interacting and thus decide how to respond. It is a valuable tool that can be used in all life situations in which we interact with others, as well as in the training situation.

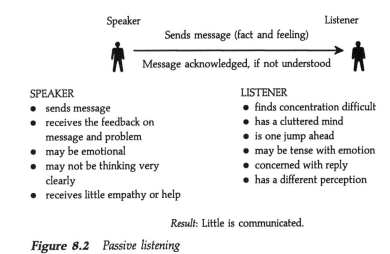

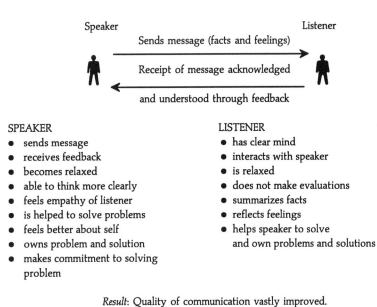

Speaker   Listener

Sends message (fact and feeling)

Message acknowledged, if not understood

SPEAKER
- sends message
- receives the feedback on message and problem
- may be emotional
- may not be thinking very clearly
- receives little empathy or help

LISTENER
- finds concentration difficult
- has a cluttered mind
- is one jump ahead
- may be tense with emotion
- concerned with reply
- has a different perception

Result: Little is communicated.

Figure 8.2 *Passive listening*

Speaker   Listener

Sends message (facts and feelings)

Receipt of message acknowledged

and understood through feedback

SPEAKER
- sends message
- receives feedback
- becomes relaxed
- able to think more clearly
- feels empathy of listener
- is helped to solve problems
- feels better about self
- owns problem and solution
- makes commitment to solving problem

LISTENER
- has clear mind
- interacts with speaker
- is relaxed
- does not make evaluations
- summarizes facts
- reflects feelings
- helps speaker to solve and own problems and solutions

Result: Quality of communication vastly improved.

Figure 8.3 *Active listening*

The originator of TA was Eric Berne, a Canadian psychotherapist, who developed his theories during the 1950s. A number of concepts expressed in distinctive jargon are associated with TA such as ego states, complementary, crossed and ulterior transactions, strokes, being OK/not OK, life scripts, games and tapes. These will be explained in this section.

TA states that we communicate from different 'ego states' of which there are three. These three ego states are **P**arent, **A**dult and **C**hild (hence PAC), which are shown as three circles arranged vertically (see

Figure 8.4). This diagram has become an internationally recognized symbol. Together, the three ego states form our personality which influences our behaviour throughout our lives. While the ego states are usually arranged as in Figure 8.4, no hierarchical significance is attached.

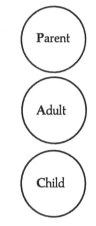

Figure 8.4   *The three ego states*

Research has indicated that throughout life our brain is like a tape recorder that operates in two main modes—record and playback. We record our life experiences on three tapes—parent, adult and child—and the strongest recordings are usually those made during our early formative years or during a significant life event. These recordings are then stored in the brain to become part of our personality and from time to time retrieved when we are subject to the right stimulus. We then make associations and we behave accordingly, i.e. the playback button is activated. How often when we hear a record, see a film, visit a place, etc., do we associate the event with good or bad memories?

No one operates constantly from the same role or state and according to TA theory it is OK to assume any of the three roles if the circumstances warrant it. Usually though, it is most appropriate and desirable to function in the adult role.

The ego states— basic structure   These represent the ways in which we react to our external world. In response to certain stimuli we may react in different ways—anxiety, fear, anger, enthusiasm—and each reaction will reflect an underlying ego state. We may, in fact, have been programmed or conditioned to respond in such a way by our life experiences.

Parent ego state   This part of our personality is derived from observing, identifying with, and often imitating our parents or those who brought us up in our formative years. We often refer to them as *role models*. Teachers and relatives also play a significant part.

This state comprises a set of attitudes, values and behaviours that we have *learnt*, consciously and unconsciously, from our role models in the past. We are acting from our parent ego state when we act in accordance with these attitudes, values and behaviours.

Adult ego state　　When we operate from this ego state we are not conditioned by our past experiences. We operate from the here and now. This part of our personality is concerned with the acquisition and processing of information. Objectivity, analysis, rationality, logic, detachment, lack of emotional involvement and impartiality are some of the words or phrases which characterize this ego state. It is this part of our personality, therefore, that we use in effective information processing, problem-solving and decision-making.

Child ego state　　This is the part of our personality that we largely learned at an early age, usually the early formative years up to the age of seven. In this ego state we are replaying behaviours, thinking and/or feelings that we *experienced* in the past. We may reveal the child aspect of our personality in a number of ways, for example, by being creative, spontaneous, self-centred, stubborn, attention seeking, cruel, by moaning, by throwing tantrums and being self indulgent. All of these are typical child-like behaviours that can, and do, surface in adult behaviour patterns.

Ego state functions　　TA theorists believe that the basic structure of three ego states which constitute our personality can be further subdivided into five major functions. There are two within the Parent, one within the Adult and two within the Child. Diagrammatically, these five functions are shown in Figure 8.5.

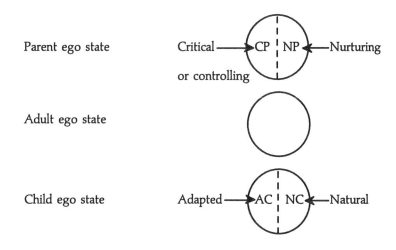

Figure 8.5　*The major functions of ego states*

Critical (or controlling) parent ego function

Parents spend a considerable amount of time controlling (and conditioning) the behaviour of their children. This is probably most obvious in the early years, although in some cases it may even accompany the child's progress into adulthood. Parents also spend quite a lot of time criticizing children's behaviour, because they want either to correct bad behaviour or to exercise control.

We have all experienced this, either as giver or receiver. In the organizational world, this function would be most apparent in a bossy and directive manager, who may invite rebellion rather than obedience from peers, subordinates or trainees.

Nurturing parent ego function

Most of us have a caring side to our nature and most of us will have been subject to a number of nurturing behaviours from our parents. It may have taken the form of being nursed through sickness, supported through a disappointment or through a stressful examination period, or simply having a cuddle. We all need both to give and receive care and attention from time to time, irrespective of age.

Adult ego function

This is the objective, rational, analytical, side of our personality that we use in a systematic way to solve problems and make decisions. Logic rather than emotions is the order of the day.

Staying perpetually in this function can make us appear cold, heartless, robotic and impersonal. While we might be effective in a problem-solving situation or doing a routine task efficiently, in a social situation we experience difficulties of familiarization and limited friendship.

The natural child ego function

This is our natural state in which we enter the world and is concerned with our uninhibited show of natural feelings. Genuine displays of friendship, affection, excitement, sadness, contentment, frustration and curiosity emanate from this function. We are at our most natural and creative in this function, but if we display this ego function too frequently, we risk being labelled immature, adolescent, childish, naïve, over-emotional and lacking in discipline.

The adapted child ego function

This function appears as a result of our conditioning at an early age. We learn that an uninhibited show of natural feelings is not always appropriate in the circumstances and so we adapt accordingly. We show we can behave correctly, often aware that such behaviour may have a 'pay-off' for us in terms of a reward. For example, parental approval for good behaviour may result in the reward of sweets or that toy we have always wanted.

Adaptation begins at a very early age and it is during this process that, in contrast with our uninhibited natural state, we are conditioned to learn feelings such as anxiety or guilt. Guilt about sex, learned in a repressive family environment, is a good example.

The PAC model and communication

TA as originally conceived by Berne focused mainly on the transactions between individuals. It was concerned with analysing the interaction between ego states of different persons.

Berne identified three main types of transaction, each with their own rules of communication.

1 Complementary transactions

A complementary transaction occurs when the ego state addressed is the ego state which responds. Two examples are given in Figures 8.6 and 8.7

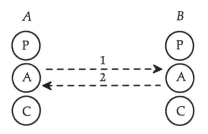

Person A speaks to the adult ego state and receives a reply from the adult ego state. The dialogue could be:

Person A: Have I explained that clearly to you?
Person B: Yes, it's fine. I now understand it.

Figure 8.6   *Complementary transactions*

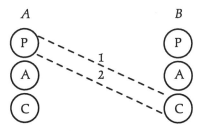

Person A speaks from the critical parent ego state to the child ego state, which responds accordingly. The dialogue could be:

Person A: You are making a terrible mess of that! I thought I'd shown you how to do it my way.
Person B: I thought I'd got the hang of it. Can you show me again?

Figure 8.7   *Complementary transactions*

Complementary transactions are OK, so interaction and communication will usually continue.

2 Crossed transactions   This occurs when the ego state addressed is not the ego state which responds. Figure 8.8 and 8.9 illustrate two examples.

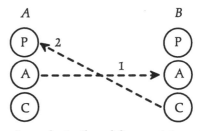

Here Person A speaks to the adult ego state and receives a response from the child ego state directed to the parent ego state. The dialogue could be:

Person A: There will be an examination on Friday.
Person B: Not another one! Well, I'm not prepared so I shan't be turning up for it.

Figure 8.8   *Crossed transactions*

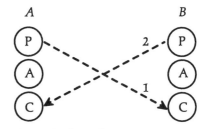

Here Person A speaks from the parent ego state addressing the child ego state and receives a response from the parent ego state addressing Person A's child ego state. The dialogue could be:

Person A: How many times have I told you to do it this way?
Person B: Well, if you were better at explaining it, I'd probably get the hang of it.

Figure 8.9   *Crossed transactions*

Crossed transactions are usually not OK and, before long, interaction and communication will cease. They will resume when a re-matching of ego states has taken place. As trainers we can:

● Choose which ego state we wish to communicate from, preferably the adult ego state.
● Consider the effect we want to have on our trainees before choosing the appropriate ego state.

Sometimes it can be appropriate to address an ego state other than the adult, such as the natural or adopted child. These latter two functions are present in all of us, and in the relaxed atmosphere of an off-site training event, far removed from the constraints of organizational life, communications which address the child ego states may, at times, be very appropriate.

3 Ulterior transactions

In most situations, relationships are usually characterized by complementary transactions. Often, however, relationships contain ulterior transactions in which there is a hidden message and the recipient needs to make use of their intuitive powers in order to pick up the full or real message. External, or behavioural signals do not really convey the deeper message.

These transactions usually involve the use of two ego states simultaneously, and this category is the basis for playing games. The use of more than two ego states simultaneously is sometimes referred to as an *angular transaction*. Such transactions are not uncommon in organizational life, but should be uncommon occurrences in the training situation where, hopefully, a positive and trusting climate exists which is conducive to learning.

An example of an ulterior transaction is illustrated in Figure 8.10, where the overt message, from Person A (manager) to Person B (subordinate) may be along the lines of 'I think your career would benefit from a new challenge' or 'I think you would welcome a change'. The ulterior message, however, could be rather different: 'I think it is time you got on your bike and went somewhere else. You are not performing'.

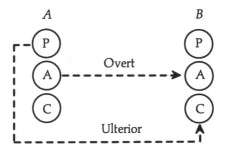

Figure 8.10   *Ulterior transactions*

Interacting with people skilled in the use of ulterior transactions is difficult and, unless the underlying concerns are brought into the open, harmonious and trusting relationships will not be established.

Strokes

Part of life's ritual involves collecting things, like stamps, and during our lifetime we collect numerous 'strokes' which, in TA terms, are *units of recognition*. The importance of strokes and the kind of strokes required varies according to our upbringing (conditioning) and our personality. In TA terms, its importance is determined by our life script.

There are three types of strokes:

1 Positive strokes This is positive feedback or 'warm fuzzies'. For example, after a training session the trainer may say, 'John, I really appreciated your contribution this morning.'

Positive strokes recognize effort, make us feel valued and secure, and increase self-esteem and confidence. In short, they make people feel good about themselves.

2 Negative strokes This is negative feedback and these are sometimes referred to as 'cold pricklies'. They could take the form of criticism, contempt, ridicule and have the opposite effect of positive strokes—they should generally be avoided.

Negative feedback can be useful if delivered constructively, but careful attention should be given to *how* it is communicated. Some tips on this are included on page 90.

Sometimes people will indulge in playing a game of collecting negative strokes for which there is usually a pay-off for the person playing it, e.g. making a point, attracting attention, getting increased peer recognition. Try to avoid getting involved unless it is necessary.

3 No strokes This is the most difficult situation to adapt to, and why solitary confinement is used as a severe punishment in penal establishments. A strokeless environment with no feedback at all will reduce self-esteem, self-confidence and an individual's value to the group. It will usually result in fall out, demotivation and the playing of games to attract attention.

'Negative feedback is better than none. I would rather have a person hate me than overlook me. As long as he hates me, I make a difference.'

M. Beattie

Conclusion Transactional Analysis has links with early learning theory and models of motivation. As a trainer, an in-depth knowledge and understanding of TA is not necessary. What is important, is an awareness of your style and its impact upon an individual or group. Some trainers, who have unwittingly adopted an inappropriate critical parent style, have often elicited adolescent behaviour from the recipients. Consequently, the focus of the course has been on playing negative games rather than on productive learning. This is one reason why those who have been in a training role and have adopted a 'schoolmaster' stance have frequently experienced problems in communicating with their learners. For the trainer, the main messages from TA are:

- We need to be aware of human conditioning and human needs.
- We need to be aware of our own mode of communication and to recognize the importance of communicating from our adult ego state.

- Recognition and feedback must be given regularly. Positive strokes develop self-esteem, increase motivation and enhance learning. By so doing, the training event does not become an arena for playing games, and time can be devoted to more positive outcomes.

Exercises

1 Consider two presenters you have observed: a good one, and one who needs to improve.

   (a) Why were they good/poor?
   (b) What did they actually do?
   (c) What have you learned from your observations?

2 What are your strengths and weaknesses in communication? What can you do to improve your weaknesses? What opportunities are there for experimentation?

3 Ask a colleague to help you improve your skills in active listening. Remember, practice makes perfect.

4 Consider a number of interactive situations you have observed that demonstrate the principles of Transactional Analysis.

   (a) What were those situations?
   (b) What form of communication was used?
   (c) What were the effects?
   (d) What have you learned?
   (e) What can you copy?

5 Think of a number of adults who regularly demonstrate one of the three different ego states. What effect did/do they have on people with whom they interact, including yourself? What can you learn from this?

6 List a number of dialogues that demonstrate complementary, crossed and ulterior transactions.

Summary

Some of the major points from this chapter are:

- Communication is a two-way process and it must be kept simple.
- We communicate far more non-verbally than we do verbally.
- Listening is an active process. It is the most used but least taught communication skill. We should regularly practise listening.
- According to Transactional Analysis (TA), we communicate from three different 'ego states'—parent, adult and child—and the adult-to-adult mode of communication is the best in most situations.
- TA emphasizes yet again the importance of positive feedback ('warm fuzzies') as a motivating tool.

Further reading

M. Argyle, *The Psychology of Interpersonal Behaviour*. Penguin Books, Harmondsworth, 1967.

M. Argyle, *Skills With People: A Guide for Managers*. Hutchinson, London, 1973.

M. Beattie, *Beyond Co-dependency*. Harper & Row, New York, 1989.

E. Berne, *Games People Play. The Psychology of Human Relationships*. Grove Press, New York, 1964.

E. Berne, *What Do You Say After You Say Hello?* Grove Press, New York, 1972; Corgi, London, 1975.

R. L. Birdwhistel, *Kinesis and Context*. Allen Lane, London, 1971.

J. Fast, *Body Language*. Souvenir Press, London, 1971.

E. T. Hall, *The Hidden Dimension*. Doubleday, New York, 1966.

T. A. Harris, *I'm OK—You're OK*. Jonathan Cape, London, 1973.

J. Hay, *Transactional Analysis for Trainers*. McGraw-Hill, Maidenhead, 1992.

A. Jay, *Effective Presentation*. British Institute of Management, Corby, 1971.

I. Mackay, *A Guide to Listening*, 2nd impression. British Association for Commercial and Industrial Education, London, 1990.

A. Mehrabian, *Tactics in Social Influence*. Prentice-Hall, Englewood Cliffs, New Jersey, 1969.

A. Mehrabian, *Silent Messages*. Wadsworth, Belmont, California, 1971.

J. Meininger, *Success through Transactional Analysis*. Grosset and Dunlop, New York, 1973.

Allan Pease, *Body Language. How to Read Others' Thoughts by their Gestures*. Sheldon Press, London, 1981.

J. N. Wismer, 'Communication effectiveness: active listening and sending feeling messages', in *The Annual Handbook for Group Facilitators* (J. W. Pfeiffer and J. E. Jones, eds). University Associates, San Diego, California, 1978.

9 Audio-visual aids

Audio-visual aids are powerful tools to help you improve your training and your delegates' learning. Competence in using them, and knowing when to use them, are some of the skills you must acquire.

At the end of this chapter you will be able to:

- identify the main types of audio-visual aid;
- list some of the main rules for use;
- use them in a competent manner.

There are many times during a training event when your verbal message can be enhanced by the use of a teaching aid. Remember that the teaching aid is not a replacement tutor. Remember also, the more complex the aid the more likely it is to go wrong and thus detract from your message.

Audio-visual aids should serve some of the following purposes:

- Highlight key points
- Illustrate complicated information
- Add variety
- Increase attention span/concentration of the learner
- Reinforce the message

Consequently they must be:

- short;
- concise;
- simple;
- easy to read/hear.

Types

Audio-visual aids can be classified accordingly:

- *Display aids*
  - chalkboards
  - wall charts
  - posters
  - flip charts
  - white boards

- *Projected aids*
  - overhead transparencies
  - films (and videos)
  - filmstrips
  - slides
  - epidiascopes

- *Three-dimensional aids*
  - actual objects
  - models
  - mock-ups

- *Duplicated or printed aids*
  - handouts
  - reading lists

- *Visual displays*
  - television
  - video discs/interactive video.

Audio aids are usually cassette recordings in their own right or an integral part of a visual aid, so that it becomes an audio-visual aid.

General rules for use

Some of these will be elaborated on in more detail later, but the following broad guidelines apply:

- Audio-visual aids should enhance the message, not detract from it. Select the media in advance that will most enhance your message.
- Keep visuals simple and uncluttered so that all members of the audience can see them.
- Check all equipment before presentation. The more technical and complicated the equipment, the more likelihood of things going wrong.
- Ensure that you are competent and confident in the use of the equipment. If in doubt, ask for a technician's help, if available.
- Use colour wherever possible.
- Assemble parts, slides, etc., in the correct order before starting.

Some major visual aids

Overhead projector

This is probably the medium you will use most. It is inexpensive, easy to use, adaptable and flexible and does not require a darkened room. Some OHPs are now very compact and portable, although these are more expensive.

Although models vary, the basic principle involves projection of an image onto a screen. On a vertical screen, a tilted beam of light produces a distortion of image ('keystone' distortion) because the

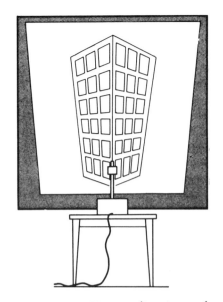

Figure 9.1 *Keystone distortion produced by an inclined beam on a vertical screen*

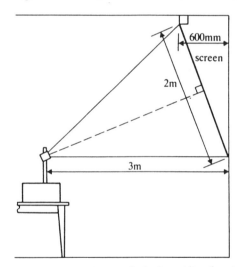

Figure 9.2 *One method of avoiding keystone distortion*
Source for the above two figures: Reproduced from *A Guide to the Overhead Projector*, by L. S. Powell, British Association for Commercial and Industrial Education, London, 3rd edition, 1980.

distance from the lens to the top edge of the screen is greater than the distance to its bottom edge (see Figure 9.1). Very often this is no great disadvantage, but there may be times when a uniformly sharp, undistorted image is necessary, then the light beam must make a right angle to the screen, as shown in Figure 9.2. Portable, tilting screens are available, but the best solution is to install a correctly angled, permanent screen surface in the room (see Figure 9.2).

When using an OHP the following hints apply:

- Check that the machine is fully operational and that you have a spare bulb. Some machines have two; so if one blows during your presentation, report the fault to a technician so that your successor may have the same insurance as you.
- Set the machine up so that it is focused with clear image (usually 2–3 m from the screen). When you start your presentation with your first transparency, you only have to switch on the machine. If possible, eliminate distortion.
- Set the screen at an angle for the audience, not straight in front (see Figure 3.9).
- Place the projector so that its glass top is at table height. If it is too high, you run the risk that it will block the audience's view of the screen.
- Have your transparencies readily at hand so that changeovers do not interrupt the flow of your presentation.
- Face the audience all the time. Do not face the screen.
- Point to relevant points of the transparency on the machine, not on the screen. This makes eye-contact with the audience easier. A pen, or special pointer, will suffice. If a laser pointer is used, then pointing to the screen is advisable. Laser pointers also give the presenter greater mobility so there is no excuse for the presenter impeding the audience's view of the screen.
- Turn off the projector when not in use. If the visual is not the current focus of attention it becomes 'visual noise' and does not enhance your message. Similarly, never leave the projector running without a visual aid.
- Show very gradually the information required. If you show the whole transparency, the audience will immediately begin to read it all. A piece of blank paper placed over or under the transparency will suffice, but masking strips can be sellotaped to the cardboard frame surrounding the transparency.
- Be conscious of where you are standing so that you do not block the view of some members of your audience. If you have set the screen at an angle to the audience you have minimized the chances of this happening.

Making transparencies   Professionally produced transparencies enhance the message and can be used many times. It is therefore worth spending time in their preparation. If they are to be used many times it is probably worth investing that little extra for professional reprographics.

In designing and producing your transparency the following tips may help:

- DO NOT use more than 4–5 words per line.
- DO NOT use more than 5–6 lines per page.
- DO NOT print vertically.

- DO use large type—normal typewriter size is too small.
- DO use colours, but never more than three or four.
- DO use good colour combinations, e.g.
  - black on clear background
  - coloured letters on clear background
  - certain combinations of colour, e.g. yellow lettering on specially made blue acetate sheets is effective.
- DO use diagrams and charts—the simpler the better. Put as much as is necessary and as little as possible on the transparency. Photocopying diagrams from books is rarely successful as they are often too complicated for a presentation.
- DO use overlays to build up a picture, but never more than four or five or picture brightness will suffer.
- DO use masking strips in your presentation to expose information gradually.
- DO use a cardboard frame. This makes handling easier and you can write your own key words on the frame as an *aide-mémoire*—another precaution that may prevent your drying up in front of the audience.
- DO use light pressure with your pens on transparencies to avoid 'blobs'. A pen with a fine point is probably best.

Flip chart   Flip charts are now almost a permanent feature of training rooms and conference facilities. They occupy very little space and are clean and tidy. Unlike an OHP transparency, sheets can be detached and displayed on the walls so that there is the opportunity to refer to points previously discussed.

When using a flip chart:

- DO NOT scribble.
- DO write tidily and in large letters so that everyone can read the message.
- DO stand to one side of the chart, not in front of it. Many of us have a 'best side' from which to write.
- DO introduce colour variation.
- DO put tops back on pens when you have used them. It increases their lifespan. And it stops you sniffing them!
- DO use a piece of paper to expose information gradually. A piece of Blu-Tack in the top two corners of a blank sheet of flip chart paper will solve the adhesion problem.
- DO prepare if you need to, and if you are going to develop your presentation in front of the audience you can lightly sketch your out-line in pencil on the flip chart—another *aide-mémoire* to insure against drying-up.

White boards   Similar guidelines apply to the use of whiteboards but the trainer must also ensure that the correct pens are available.

Some training rooms have an electronic white board which enables whatever has been recorded on the board to be photoreduced, photocopied and the required number of copies duplicated. While these handouts will not be professionally produced there are a few advantages of using such a facility:

- They record the 'here and now' deliberations of the group, supplying them with immediate handouts which provide immediate reinforcement to learning.
- They often record some excellent material that can be used at future training events and from which others can benefit. They can, therefore, become incorporated in new or improved handouts for future use.

Samples and models   The use of samples and models needs careful preparation, but they do add interest and give people a sense of reality in that they may be examples of actual things they will be dealing with. They also increase audience participation as samples have to be passed around the room and they therefore tend to bring an atmosphere of informality into the proceedings.

The main problem is to have a reasonable ratio of participants to samples. A limited number of samples with a large group can mean long periods of idleness for participants, loss of interest and waste of time. Dividing the group into sub-groups may get round this problem.

Slide and film projectors   The use of projectors in training always adds a professional touch, brings a sense of fun to the proceedings and increases the anticipation of the group.

As both types involve quite sophisticated equipment, the chances of something going wrong are increased. Double-check beforehand that everything works—your message and your credibility could suffer badly if not.

Slides must be pre-arranged in the proper order in the holding device of the slide projector (usually 35 mm). You should rehearse your presentation before the training event to make sure that the slides are in the correct order and are arranged properly (not sideways, upside down or backwards).

The same rules that apply to OHP transparencies also apply to slides. The two main drawbacks in the use of slides are that equipment and production costs are greater and that the room generally must be darkened to show them. Gauging audience reaction is therefore more difficult, as is audience participation.

Handouts   Handouts are useful for:

- reinforcing the main points of the presentation;
- providing the audience with reference material for further study.

A problem facing many trainers is when to distribute the material—

before or after the presentation. There are advantages and disadvantages with both.

Before presentation
Advantage: offers a guide to work through for speaker, a structure for the audience
Disadvantage: audience read handout and fail to concentrate on speaker.

After presentation
Advantage: does not distract from speaker
Disadvantage: audience do not read it because they have already listened to what has been said.

There is no easy answer, but many trainers prefer to distribute *after* the presentation and use the handouts to reinforce the message.

Other visual aids   In recent years more sophisticated hardware has been used in training situations.

1   CCTV systems—specialist equipment, expensive and requires technical expertise and confidence in its use.
2   Computer-based training—requires expensive equipment and specialist experience.
3   Video disc—requires expensive equipment and specialist expertise. Sometimes used with computers as interactive video.

All of these require advanced knowledge and experience in their use and lengthy training is usually required to achieve competence, or specialist expertise is contracted-in.

CBT and interactive video are sophisticated and expensive forms of open learning that were discussed in Chapter 6. An in-depth discussion of these media is beyond the scope of this work. Readers are advised to consult other publications in the current series which have a more extensive coverage of these subjects.

Exercises   1   List some of the things you do well in using audio-visual aids.
2   List some of the areas for improvement.
3   List three individuals you have observed who have used visual aids.
    (a)   What was the situation?
    (b)   Which visual aids did they use?
    (c)   What did they do well? Why?
    (d)   What did they do poorly? Why?
    (e)   What can you imitate, or ensure you don't do, in order to improve your own performance?

Summary

Some of the major points from this chapter are:

- Audio-visual aids should enhance your message, not detract from it. You should only use them for this purpose, not as gimmicks.
- Many audio-visual aids require some technical competence and familiarity. Ensure that everything is in working order before use in front of a group.

Further reading

T. Bentley, *Training to Meet the Technology Challenge*. McGraw-Hill, Maidenhead, 1992.

C. Dean and Q. Whitlock, *A Handbook of Computer Based Training*. Kogan Page, London, 1989.

H. Ellington, *Producing Teaching Materials: A Handbook for Teachers and Trainers*. Kogan Page, London, 1985.

D. Flegg and J. McHale, *Selecting and Using Training Aids*. Kogan Page, London, 1991.

M. Picciotto, I. Robertson and R. Colley, *Interactivity: Designing and Using Interactive Video*. Kogan Page, London, 1989.

L. S. Powell, *A Guide to the Overhead Projector*. BACIE, London, 1964.

L. S. Powell, *A Guide to the Use of Visual Aids*. BACIE, London, 1978.

A. J. Romiszowski, *The Selection and Use of Instructional Media. For Improved Classroom Teaching and for Interactive Individualised Instruction* (2nd edn). Kogan Page, London, 1988.

10 Evaluation of training

Evaluation is the fifth and final stage in the training cycle, the most neglected and perhaps the most important. It is necessary to improve your own performance, your delegates' learning and the course itself.

At the end of this chapter you will be able to:

- state the main purposes of evaluation;
- identify the three main types of evaluation;
- carry out some of the necessary steps in the main types of evaluation.

The term 'evaluation' is widely used and definitions and perceptions vary. It sometimes overlaps with such terms as 'validation' and 'assessment', which can confuse the situation.

It would probably help to define evaluation in the broadest sense; to take Goldstein's definition:

Evaluation is the systematic collection of descriptive and judgmental information necessary to make effective training decisions related to the selection, adoption, value and modification of various instructional activities.

Purposes of evaluation

Evaluation is the fifth stage in the training cycle. It forms an integral part of the systematic approach, the quality control part, and therefore should not—as it often is—be neglected. The main purposes of evaluation can be summarized as follows:

1. It provides feedback on how well you are doing. This not only includes your own performance, but gives you information on the quality of the design and delivery of training activities. It can focus on the whole as well as the part and provides useful feedback for the 'Review to improve' stage.

   In the same way that we provide feedback through various mechanisms to our learners, we also can receive it to help improve our performance and our product.

2. It can add to the body of knowledge on training principles and practice that could have a much wider application than feedback evaluation.

We can learn from the evaluation process and the techniques used and possibly refine or improve those techniques as well as seeing opportunities to apply them in other fields.

3 It can measure the effectiveness of the transfer of learning back to the workplace. This can be a more lengthy, and therefore expensive, process and a cost-benefit analysis is required before such an operation can be started.

4 It can relate our training policy and practice to organizational goals. Is the form and content of training consistent with company philosophy and culture? Will it contribute to organizational development over the next few years? Is it the most cost-effective way of achieving these wider objectives?

When one moves to the wider field it is more difficult to obtain precise measurements but it can be a very valuable process. Apart from the collection of valuable data, the process at in-company level can improve communications between the training department and the rest of the organization, as well as raise the profile and the quality of interaction.

The objective of this book is to help trainers to improve their training competence. Consequently, this chapter will not focus on the wider, organizational perspective but on feedback evaluation with a view to improving trainer competence, and improving the course in order to meet learning objectives. With the latter in mind, a short section on testing has been included.

Types of evaluation

Evaluation can be divided into three types, although there is some overlap and all three are necessary to provide effective evaluation. In outline, the three main types are given below.

1 *Self-evaluation.* This will help us improve our effectiveness as trainers. We can critique ourselves, we can ask for a critique from our learners and we can request a critique from our colleagues. The last is not always possible, but if you are working in a team-teaching situation valuable information can be forthcoming and it can make a substantial contribution towards developing your competence. Asking for evaluation from others, especially from your learners, can be a revealing process. New trainers may not be ready to go through such an ordeal, so think carefully before you try it. Tools to assist in this process will be discussed later.

2 *Learner evaluation.* This is the process by which your learners record their thoughts, comments and observations about the training. This could be directed at the trainers as well as the training programme.

3 *Testing.* This is the process of obtaining a measurement of whether or not the learners learned what was intended. Sometimes we can test orally with questions; other times we need to employ tests in which the delegates write. We need to decide both *what* we shall test and *how* we shall test it.

Measuring knowledge and skill acquisition is relatively easy. Measuring attitude changes and on-the-job behavioural changes that result from training is much more difficult. Whatever we test, some knowledge of test construction and validation principles is required and, as a general rule, the more complex the learning we are measuring, the more difficult and more refined the process needs to become.

Self-evaluation

This is not an easy process and requires a firm commitment to be honest with oneself and to improve and become more competent. Objectivity is also a problem, and this becomes difficult with the passing of time.

It is, therefore, important to not only critique oneself at the end of a training event, but also periodically during the event—perhaps at the end of each day and occasionally at the end of each session.

One way of making the self-evaluation less subjective and more objective is to use a questionnaire that is completed by self, learners and colleagues. It requires risk-taking but it can pay considerable dividends. It also gives the opportunity to check out your own perceptions with others, heightens your awareness of strengths so you can play to them in future, and highlights development points.

Self-evaluation checklist

Directions: Indicate your answer to each question below by placing a tick ($\sqrt{}$) in the appropriate column. Areas in need of improvement will be identified by ticks in the 'Sometimes' and 'No' columns. There is room at the end to list your action plans.

	Yes	Some-times	No
1 Did I utilize the suggested course of study?	....	....	....
2 Did I ensure my material was appropriate for the group?	....	....	....
3 Was my material well organized?	....	....	....
4 Did I seek assistance in planning and implementing the course?	....	....	....
5 Were the objectives clearly stated to the participants?	....	....	....
6 Did I achieve the objectives?	....	....	....
7 Did I set the scene and 'break the ice' effectively?	....	....	....
8 Did I keep my course outline up-to-date?	....	....	....
9 Did I make allowances within the course outline to cope with individual differences?	....	....	....
10 Did I modify the course to meet individual needs?	....	....	....
11 Did I prepare session plans?	....	....	....

12 Did I give each delegate the attention he or she needed? ....

13 Did I use methods and techniques appropriate for the presentation? ....

14 Did I evaluate my sessions for:
  (a) the appropriateness of the objectives? ....
  (b) the appropriateness of the learning methods? ....
  (c) the utilization of learning aids especially visual aids? ....
  (d) the organization of the subject matter? ....
  (e) the use made of time available? ....
  (f) the consideration of individual differences? ....
  (g) the amount of group participation? ....
  (h) the amount of individual participation? ....
  (i) the depth of my knowledge of the subject matter? ....

15 During my presentations did I:
  (a) structure them clearly? ....
  (b) ensure that my speech was clear and audible? ....
  (c) maintain good eye contact? ....
  (d) use appropriate language? ....
  (e) convey enthusiasm? ....
  (f) involve the audience? ....
  (g) make good use of visual aids? ....
  (h) use appropriate body language? ....

16 Did I encourage group members to develop and experiment with their own ideas? ....

17 Did I have a good rapport with the group? ....

18 Did the course members feel free to ask questions? ....

19 Did I listen effectively? ....

20 Did I motivate the delegates to engage in related out-of-class activities? ....

21 Did I ensure that the physical arrangements were satisfactory? ....

22 Did I communicate our needs to the host centre? ....

23 Did I maintain a good relationship with the host centre and with the support staff? ....

24 Did I give learners the opportunity to evaluate the course? ....

25 Did I ensure that the standard and presentation of my handouts were appropriate? ....

Action plan   Some of the things I did well were:

Some of the things I need to improve on are:

What I will do to ensure that I improve:

Facilitator   *Directions*: For each item listed, place a tick ($\checkmark$) in the appropriate
evaluation checklist   column that best describes in your opinion the facilitator/tutor/trainer.
Be honest but not vindictive.

NB This could also be completed by your colleagues(s) in the training
team.

	Excellent	Satis-factory	Room for improve-ment
1 Knows subject thoroughly.	....	....	....
2 Uses material that is appropriate to the group.	....	....	....
3 Gives the impression of being well organized.	....	....	....
4 Makes one feel welcome and at ease.	....	....	....
5 Shows a good rapport with group.	....	....	....
6 Speaks clearly.	....	....	....
7 Shows enthusiasm and enjoyment for the job.	....	....	....
8 Is well prepared.	....	....	....
9 Displays concern and understanding for individuals.	....	....	....

	Excellent	Satis-factory	Room for improve-ment
10 Uses tact and diplomacy when dealing with delegates.	....	....	....
11 Exercises appropriate management of the group and the learning activities.	....	....	....
12 Praises good work and accomplishments.	....	....	....
13 Corrects individual mistakes tactfully.	....	....	....
14 Encourages individuals to ask questions and participate in sessions.	....	....	....
15 Uses a variety of learning methods.	....	....	....
16 Gives clear and concise explanations and briefings.	....	....	....
17 Relates well to his/her colleagues in the training team.	....	....	....
18 During presentations:			
(a) structures them clearly	....	....	....
(b) ensures speech is clear and audible	....	....	....
(c) uses appropriate body language	....	....	....
(d) conveys enthusiasm	....	....	....
(e) involves the group	....	....	....
(f) makes good use of visual aids	....	....	....
19 Listens effectively and checks for understanding.	....	....	....
20 Distributes handouts of appropriate quality.	....	....	....
21 Gives the opportunity for feedback and evaluation.	....	....	....
22 Establishes good relationship with the host centre and the support staff.	....	....	....
23 Manages the whole event with an easy competence.	....	....	....
24 Encourages experimentation and individual contributions.	....	....	....
25 Values the group as people.	....	....	....

Action plan   Some of things I do well are:

Some of things I need to improve on are:

What I will do to ensure I improve:

If you have used both the self-evaluation checklist and the facilitator evaluation checklist, compare the two. Check out your perceptions and then finalize your action plan.

Do not lose sight of all the things you do well. These you repeat and keep in your repertoire.

Learner evaluation

In the last section, the learners had the opportunity to evaluate the facilitator. They must also have the opportunity to evaluate the product, i.e. the course workshop, etc., as their comments provide invaluable information, not only on how the course met their needs, but also on how the course can be improved for future participants. Such feedback is especially important with a new course, but should also be received with a well-established course—not only to guard against complacency and staleness but to check if needs have changed. Training is a dynamic entity and can never stand still.

Below is a typical evaluation form. It can be used at the end of a training course, at the end of a major segment or after one session if such a session is new or has been considerably revised. Do not overdo the use of the form otherwise you risk alienating your learners.

Learner's course evaluation

Course:.....................................   *Name* (optional): ....
Date:...   *Job title* (optional):............................
                                       Trainer(s):.......................................

Below are a series of questions appertaining to the course. Please respond to each by circling the appropriate number from 1 to 5.

1	The course objectives were clearly explained.	5 4 3 2 1	The course objectives were not explained.
2	The course objectives were consistent with my needs and abilities.	5 4 3 2 1	The course objectives were not consistent with my needs and abilities.
3	The methods used were appropriate to meet course objectives.	5 4 3 2 1	The methods used were inappropriate to meet course objectives.
4	The course was well structured.	5 4 3 2 1	The course was poorly structured.
5	The course introduced me to a lot of new knowledge.	5 4 3 2 1	The course taught me nothing new.
6	There was plenty of opportunity for reinforcement of learning.	5 4 3 2 1	There was no opportunity for reinforcement of learning.
7	The course was appropriate for this group in terms of: (a) content (b) method.	5 4 3 2 1	The course was inappropriate for this group in terms of: (a) content (b) method.
8	I felt motivated to learn more.	5 4 3 2 1	I felt unmotivated to learn more.
9	The course content was closely related to objectives.	5 4 3 2 1	The course content was unrelated to objectives.
10	The visual aids were used well and assisted my learning.	5 4 3 2 1	The visual aids were used poorly and did not assist my learning.
11	The standard of presentation was high.	5 4 3 2 1	The standard of presentation was poor.
12	The course handouts were of a very high standard.	5 4 3 2 1	The course handouts were of a poor standard.
13	The course handouts reinforced my learning.	5 4 3 2 1	The course handouts did nothing to help my learning.
14	The atmosphere in the group was very conducive to learning.	5 4 3 2 1	The atmosphere in the group hindered my learning.

15 The tasks presented had practical relevance.   5 4 3 2 1   The tasks presented had no practical relevance.

16 I always felt my questions were fully answered.   5 4 3 2 1   I never felt my questions were answered.

17 I always felt I could contribute my experience.   5 4 3 2 1   I never felt I could contribute my experience.

18 The administrative arrangements were excellent and contributed to the success of the course.   5 4 3 2 1   The administrative arrangements were poor and made no positive contribution to the course success.

19 The training and/or conference facilities were excellent.   5 4 3 2 1   The training and/or conference facilities were poor.

20 The time allocation for the course was perfect.   5 4 3 2 1   The time allocation for the course was inappropriate.

21 The trainer(s) gave me the support I needed to learn.   5 4 3 2 1   The trainer(s) gave me little support to assist my learning.

22 Much of the learning can be taken away and applied.   5 4 3 2 1   I have learned nothing of relevance or practical application.

23 The most useful parts of the course were:

24 The least useful parts of the course were:

25 To improve the course further I would suggest the following:

Thank you for completing the form. Your comments are greatly appreciated.

Learning and action plans   On training courses it is important to keep at the back of the delegate's mind the real world and what learnings they are going to transfer from the course.

A useful way of doing this and of reinforcing learning is to conduct a learning review at the end of each day. Delegates are asked to record on paper at least three things they have learned during the day and which are probably of use back in the real world. Delegates are then asked to share this with the rest of group.

This is a very useful process. It gives feedback on learning and progress on a daily basis to tutors and course members and keeps a focus on transferring learning. As the course proceeds the delegates build up a large learning log and this can then form the basis of their action plan.

The formal action plan is produced towards the end of the course from the learning log as follows:

1 Learning is grouped in a meaningful way.
2 Tasks are identified and prioritized.
3 Methods of implementation are considered.
4 A realistic time frame is decided (usually no more than six months).

A very useful process at this stage is to institute a co-counselling network in which each participant can be helped by another course member either to finalize the action plan or simply just to share it and receive some kind of feedback. If the group have been together for a reasonable period of time and has matured, members should be very amenable to such a process and should learn from the experiences.

The action plan is a positive commitment on the part of the individual to post-course follow-up action. It also forms an excellent basis for follow-up, which could either be with the trainers (easier if they are internal) or with the sponsoring manager at work.

Trainers can discuss with delegate and/or manager the extent to which the action plan has been implemented and why there has been success and failure. They can also receive feedback on the benefits to the organization accruing from the action plan and therefore, indirectly, some indication of how the course met individual, departmental and organizational needs.

Testing

Much training, particularly in the management development field, does not involve testing. On many other courses it is an important part of the proceedings. Tests have three main uses:

1 to evaluate the achievements of the delegates;
2 to measure the effectiveness of the training *re* your tuition;
3 to locate errors and weaknesses that need correction.

In general any test that you develop and/or use should be:

1 valid, i.e. measure what it is supposed to measure;
2 reliable, i.e. will give consistently the same result no matter who administers or scores it;
3 usable in your situation.

NB A test may be excellent, but if it takes too long to administer or is impossible to score with the measuring devices available, then it is not usable. It is part of your role to exercise sound, professional judgement about the best tool for the job.

Tests fall into two major categories:

1 Performance tests
2 Knowledge tests

Performance tests   These measure skills. In its truest form, a performance test is a one-to-one situation where the trainer carefully evaluates a single individual as a task or series of tasks is accomplished. Driving a car or flying an aircraft (simulator or for real), are good examples. It is an excellent way of finding out exactly what an individual can do, but it is very time-consuming if it has to be applied to each individual in the group.

Performance tests need to be carefully planned and when preparing such a test you must ensure that you:

- determine exactly the elements you wish to test;
- list the operations and/or steps;
- establish acceptable standards for each element being tested as well as the relative value of each element;
- prepare instructions, preferably written;
- develop a scoring sheet that will provide a standardized guide when observing and evaluating individuals;
- list and have available all equipment needed to perform the test.

Knowledge tests   There are two main types of knowledge test: subjective and objective. The former is the essay-type test and is not often used in training situations, mainly because of problems of standardization and gradings.

There are, however, several types of objective tests and if you are going to use them you should have carried out the following:

- Know exactly what it is you intend to teach and the results you hope to achieve.
- Know the importance of the material you select for testing in relation to the overall course objectives. This involves working out the value or importance of the parts to the whole.
- Prioritize the items selected for testing, giving them a proportionate part of the total test, i.e. the most important parts form a larger proportion of the test.

The various types of objective test are briefly outlined below.

Oral   These are usually used for pre-testing or review and their preparation requires the same attention to detail as a written test. In each case you need to determine in advance what the possible range of correct answers will be for each question. You will then know how to react to what you hear or see.

Completion   These require individuals to finish a statement or drawing and this type of test represents a compromise between the recall of an essay and the 50–50 chance of a good guess provided by the true–false question. Do not be surprised by the variety of correct answers you can get for questions that you were certain only had one answer. Hence the need to continually refine the questions. Thus only tasks that require simple calculations or verbal associations should be tested with a completed question. The search for such questions will often cause you to concentrate on detail, and therefore you should limit the use of this type of question to the testing of bits of information and specific facts.

Multiple choice　This consists of an introductory sentence or incomplete statement with four or more suggested answers. The object is to choose the best or nearest-correct response. In this way you avoid the requirement of an answer that is absolutely true in all circumstances and reduce the opportunities for respondents to introduce different replies to those you are expecting. The guessing factor is considerably reduced with multiple-choice questioning, especially if four or five responses are provided. For a 10-item, four-response, multiple-choice test the probability of obtaining a score of 70 per cent on the basis of guesswork alone is 1 in 1000. When this is coupled with a large sample of content, the multiple-choice test is a very useful test of knowledge.

Matching　This usually consists of a list of questions with a list of possible answers for every question. The object is to choose an answer for each question. A lot of material can be covered with this type of test. The guessing factor is small and the scoring is simple and objective.

True–false　This test consists of statements to be judged true or false and answered 'yes' or 'no'. A large number of items can be answered and scored in a short period of time, so a wide sampling of material is possible. When a scoring key is used there is no difference of opinion as to the correct answer and the scoring is speeded up.

True–false tests are useful for testing pieces of information and specific facts. The main problems are:

- Very few statements can be made that can be answered with a definite 'yes' or 'no'. Very few issues are black and white—there are usually 'shades of grey' in between. Thus many subjects to be tested do not lend themselves to the true–false form of questioning.
- The questions have to be carefully written so they are not misinterpreted.
- The chance of getting a correct answer through guessing is 50 per cent. On a 10-item, true–false test the chance of answering 70 per cent of questions correctly through guesswork is 1 in 6.

All these types of test serve as a tool to help the trainer evaluate knowledge learning. Administering these tests is as much a test of your competence to impart knowledge as it is of your students' ability to assimilate knowledge.

Detailed information and advice on test design and construction is beyond the scope of this book. Your local reference library or Social Sciences or Education Department library at a university should have a wealth of information on this.

Exercises

1 List a number of courses in which you have been involved.
   (a) What types of evaluation did you carry out?
   (b) What were the outcomes?
   (c) What aspects can be improved upon?
   (d) What could you implement?
2 Have you ever received evaluations on yourself as a trainer? What feedback was positive? What areas do you need to work on to improve?
3 Are there any courses in which you will be involved in the future? If so, what type of evaluation will you carry out?

Summary

The main points from this chapter are:

- Evaluation is a constant process and is the fifth stage in the training cycle.
- Evaluation can help you improve your own competence as a trainer as well as improve the quality of the course.
- Learning reviews and action planning reinforce learning, increase the likelihood of transfer of learning and give further information on the effectiveness of training.
- Testing is a useful method of evaluating student learning as well as your ability to impart relevant knowledge and train in appropriate skills.
- There are numerous types of objective tests suitable to evaluate learning.

Further reading

P. Bramley, *Evaluating Training Effectiveness. Translating Theory Into Practice* (2nd edn). McGraw-Hill, Maidenhead, 1995.

M. Easterby-Smith, *Evaluating Management Developments, Training and Education* (2nd edn). Gower, Aldershot, 1994.

I. L. Goldstein, 'Training in work organization', *Annual Review of Psychology*, 1980, pp 220–72.

A. C. Hamblin, *Evaluation and Control of Training*. McGraw-Hill, Maidenhead, 1974.

T. Jackson, *Evaluation: Relating Training to Business Performance*. Kogan Page, London, 1989.

D. L. Kirkpatrick, 'Evaluation of training', in *Training and Development Handbook*. (R. L. Craig and L. R. Bittel, eds). McGraw-Hill, New York, 1967.

A. C. Newby, *Training Evaluation Handbook*. Gower, Aldershot, 1992.

J. Phillips, *Handbook of Training Evaluation and Measurement Methods* (2nd edn). Kogan Page, London, 1991.

D. Reay, *Evaluating Training*. Kogan Page, London, 1994.

P. Warr, M. Bird and N. Rackham, *Evaluation of Management Training*. Gower, Aldershot, 1970.

Appendix: Beyond this book

A book should not be an end in itself. While it should increase your knowledge, its main contribution should be in helping you put into practice your learning. Keep your own situation to the forefront of your mind—while only *you* can do that, and only *you* can implement your learning, both *you* and *others* benefit from this process.

Here are a number of ways/suggestions to help you implement your learning. This is a suggested framework only, so feel free to adopt and change it in any way that suits you.

PART I

1 Some of the major learning points for me from this book are: ...
2 Some of the learning points that I could implement are: ...
3 In order of priority, the learning points which I am going to implement are: ...
4 For each action point on my list, I must now decide:

Action Point	How I am going to implement	When I am going to implement
....	....	....
....	....	....

To help me action these points, I may need to answer the following questions:

1 The factors that will help me are: ...
2 The factors that will hinder me are: ...
3 The kind of supports I need are: ...
4 The people from whom I want these supports are: ...

GOOD LUCK!

PART II

Here are 12 suggested activities to help you develop as a trainer. Some of them could be integrated into Part I.

1 Be aware of my strengths but recognize that I never stop learning.
2 Experiment with one new method on my next course.
3 Introduce at least one new element into a course every time I deliver it.
4 Take the opportunity to observe someone else in the training situation.
5 Take the opportunity to co-facilitate with different people.
6 Make a contract with myself and my boss for a number of days for personal development every year. (Remember, that going on a course gives you insight into what it is like on the other side of the desk.)
7 Join a reference group of practitioners in the same field—locally or nationally—and discuss my work and hear about theirs.
8 Be aware of the literature in my field and continually update. Read one new book every three months.
9 Subscribe to relevant journals in my field and read them.
10 Draw up a learning log to record my observations and learning after

(a) every session;
(b) every training day;
(c) every training course.

With every learning point, consider *how* and *when* you can implement. Use the guide in Part I of this appendix if appropriate.
11 Write about my own experiences and share them with others.
12 Give of myself unselfishly to all situations—that usually guarantees I will get more back!

Please send me further information of the range of Training and Development services available. I am particularly interested in:

☐ Management Training Courses

☐ Management Development Consultancy

☐ Psychometric Testing

☐ Counselling Services

Signed: ....

Position: ....

Company: ....

Address: ....

....

....

Telephone no: .... Fax no:................................

Please mail to:

Administration Manager
Heyford Associates
Heyford House
Nether Heyford
Northampton
NN7 3NN
United Kingdom

Telephone: + 44 - (0)1327–342339

Fax: + 44 - (0)1327–349389

HEYFORD ASSOCIATES

Bibliography

H. Alder, *The Right Brain Manager*. Piatkus, London, 1993.

H. Alder, *NLP: The New Art and Science of Getting What You Want*. Piatkus, London, 1994.

C. P. Alderfer, *Existence, Relatedness & Growth*. Free Press, New York, 1972.

American Society for Training and Development, *The Past, Present, and Future of Workplace Learning*. American Society for Training and Development, Alexandria, Virginia, 1994.

M. Argyle, *The Psychology of Interpersonal Behaviour*. Penguin Books, Harmondsworth, 1967.

M. Argyle, *Skills With People: A Guide for Managers*. Hutchinson, London, 1973.

B. Auvine, B. Densmore, M. Extrom, S. Poole and M. Shanklin, *A Manual for Group Facilitators*. Center for Conflict Resolution, Center for Conflict Resolution, Madison, Wisconsin, 1977.

R. Bandler and J. Grinder, *Frogs into Princes*. Real People Press, London, 1979.

M. Barca and K. Cobb, *Beginnings and Endings*. Gower, Aldershot, 1994.

S. Bartram and B. Gibson, *Activities for Developing Training Skills*. Gower, Aldershot, 1994.

M. Beattie, *Beyond Co-dependency*. Harper & Row, New York, 1989.

R. Bennett (ed.), 'The right role', in *Improving Trainer Effectiveness*. Gower, Aldershot, 1988.

E. Berne, *Games People Play. The Psychology of Human Relationships*. Grove Press, New York, 1964.

E. Berne, *What Do You Say After You Say Hello?* Grove Press, New York, 1972; Corgi, London, 1975.

T. Bentley, *Training to Meet the Technology Challenge*. McGraw-Hill, Maidenhead, 1992.

T. Bentley, *Facilitation, Providing Opportunities for Learning*. McGraw-Hill, Maidenhead, 1994.

R. L. Birdwhistel, *Kinesis and Context*. Allen Lane, London, 1971.

T. Bourner, V. Martin and P. Race, *Workshops That Work. 100 Ideas to Make your Training Events More Effective*. McGraw-Hill, Maidenhead, 1993.

P. Bramley, *Evaluating Training Effectiveness. Translating Theory Into Practice* (2nd edn). McGraw-Hill, Maidenhead, 1995.

S. Brookfield, *Understanding and Facilitating Adult Learning: A Comprehensive Guide to Principles and Effective Practices*. Jossey Bass, San Francisco, 1976.

D. Cartwright, 'The nature of group cohesiveness', in *Group Dynamics Research and Theory* (D. Cartwright and A. Zander, eds). Harper & Row, New York, 1968.

J. Constable and R. McCormick, *The Making of British Managers*. BIM & CBI, London, 1987.

Coopers & Lybrand Associates, *Challenge to Complacency*. Training Commission, Sheffield, 1985.

D. Coupland, *Generation X*. Abacus, London, 1994.

A. Cowling, M. J. K. Stanworth, R. D. Bennett, J. Curran and P. Lyons, *Behavioural Sciences for Managers* (2nd edn). Arnold, London, 1988.

I. K. Davies, *Instructional Technique*. McGraw-Hill, New York, 1981.

C. Dean and Q. Whitlock, *A Handbook of Computer Based Training*. Kogan Page, London, 1989.

A. I. S. Debenham, *A Training Officer's Guide for Discussion Leading* (6th impression). BACIE, London, 1981.

R. Dilts, *Applications of Neuro-Linguistic Programming*. Meta Publications, Cupertino, California, 1983.

T. Douglas, *Groups—Understanding People Gathered Together*. Tavistock Publications, London and New York, 1983.

M. Easterby-Smith, *Evaluating Management Developments, Training and Education* (2nd edn). Gower, Aldershot, 1994.

H. Ellington, E. Addinall and F. Percival, *A Handbook of Game Design*. Kogan Page, London, 1982.

H. Ellington, *Producing Teaching Materials: A Handbook for Teachers and Trainers*. Kogan Page, London, 1985.

J. Fast, *Body Language*. Souvenir Press, London, 1971.

D. Flegg and J. McHale, *Selecting and Using Training Aids*. Kogan Page, London, 1991.

J. Fripp, *Learning Through Simulations. A Guide to the Design and Use of Simulations in Business and Education*. McGraw-Hill, Maidenhead, 1993.

J. Gentry (ed.), *A Guide to Business Gaming and Experiential Learning*. Kogan Page, London, 1990.

I. L. Goldstein, 'Training in work organization', *Annual Review of Psychology*, 1980, pp. 220–272.

E. T. Hall, *The Hidden Dimension*. Doubleday, New York, 1966.

A. C. Hamblin, *Evaluation and Control of Training*. McGraw-Hill, Maidenhead, 1974.

C. Handy et al., *The Making of Managers: A Report on Management Education, Training and Development in USA, West Germany, France, Japan and the UK*. NEDO, MSC & BIM, London, 1987.

T. A. Harris, *I'm OK—You're OK*. Johnathan Cape, London, 1973.

T. L. Harris and W. E. Schwahn, *Selected Readings on the Learning Process*. Oxford University Press, New York, 1961.

L. Hart, *Faultless Facilitation*. Kogan Page, London, 1992.

D. Hawkridge, W. Newton and C. Hall, *Computers in Company Training*. Routledge, London, 1988.

J. Hay, *Transactional Analysis for Trainers*. McGraw-Hill, Maidenhead, 1992.

J. Heider, *The Tao of Leadership*. Wildwood House, Aldershot, 1986.

J. Heron, *Facilitators Handbook*. Kogan Page, London, 1989.

J. Heron, *Group Facilitation. Theories and Models For Practice*. Kogan Page, London, 1993.

F. Hertzberg, *Work and the Nature of Man*. World Publishing Co., Cleveland, Ohio, 1966.

B. Hodgson, *Key Terms and Issues in Open and Distance Learning*. Kogan Page, London, 1993.

P. Honey and A. Mumford, *A Manual of Learning Styles*. Peter Honey, Maidenhead, 1982.

P. Honey and A. Mumford, *Using Your Learning Styles* (2nd edn). Peter Honey, Maidenhead, 1986.

G. Houston, *The Red Book of Groups and How to Lead Them Better*. Rochester Foundation, 1984.

T. Jackson, *Evaluation: Relating Training to Business Performance*. Kogan Page, London, 1989.

D. Jacques, *Learning In Groups* (2nd edn). Kogan Page, London, 1991.

A. Jay, *Effective Presentation*. Management Publications, 1971.

J. E. Jones, 'Dealing with disruptive individuals in meetings', in *The 1980 Annual Handbook for Group Facilitators* (J. W. Pfeiffer and J. W. Jones, eds). University Associates, San Diego, California, 1980.

K. Jones, *A Handbook for Teachers and Trainers*. Kogan Page, London, 1982.

K. Jones, *A Sourcebook of Management Simulations*. Kogan Page, London, 1989.

K. Jones, *Imaginative Events. A Sourcebook of Innovative Simulations, Exercises, Puzzles and Games* Vols 1 and 2. McGraw-Hill, Maidenhead, 1992.

A. Kirby, *Games for Trainers* Vols 1 and 2. Gower, Aldershot, 1992.

A. Kirby, *Games for Trainers* Vol. 3. Gower, Aldershot, 1994.

A. Kirby, *A Compendium of Icebreakers, Energisers and Introductions*. Gower, Aldershot, 1993.

D. L. Kirkpatrick, 'Evaluation of training', in *Training and Development Handbook* (R. L. Craig and L. R. Bittel, eds). McGraw-Hill, New York, 1967.

H. Knowles and M. Knowles, *Introduction to Group Dynamics* (2nd edn). Association Press/Follett, Chicago, 1972.

M. S. Knowles, *Self-Directed Learning*. Association Press/Follett, Chicago, 1975.

M. S. Knowles, *The Modern Practice of Adult Education. From Pedagogy to Andragogy*. Follett, Chicago, 1980.

M. S. Knowles, *The Adult Learner: A Neglected Species* (3rd edn). Gulf Publishing Co., 1984.

D. A. Kolb and R. Fry, 'Towards an applied theory of experiential learning', in *Theories of Group Process* (C. L. Cooper, ed.) Wiley, New York, 1975.

C. P. Ladousse, *Role Play*. Oxford University Press, 1987.

D. Leigh, *A Practical Approach to Group Training*. Kogan Page, London, 1991.

A. H. Maslow, *Motivation and Personality* (2nd edn). Harper & Row, New York, 1954.

D. McClelland, J. W. Atkinson, R. A. Clarke and F. A. Lowell, *The Achievement Motive*. Irvington Publishers, New York, 1976.

D. C. McGregor, *The Human Side of Enterprise*. McGraw-Hill, New York, 1960.

A. Mehrabian, *Tactics in Social Influence*. Prentice Hall, Englewood Cliffs, New Jersey, 1969.

A. Mehrabian, *Silent Messages*. Wadsworth, Belmont, California, 1971.

J. Meininger, *Success through Transactional Analysis*. Grosset and Dunlop, New York, 1973.

Morry van Ments, *The Effective Use of Role Play. A Handbook for Teachers and Trainers* (revised edn). Kogan Page, London, 1989.

Morry van Ments, *Active Talk. The Effective Use of Discussion in Learning*. Kogan Page, London, 1990.

E. Milroy, *Role Play: A Practical Guide*. Aberdeen University Press, Aberdeen, 1982.

A. Mumford, *Making Experience Pay*. McGraw-Hill, Maidenhead, 1980.

L. Nadler, 'The variety of training roles', *Industrial and Commercial Training*, 1969, Vol. 1, No. 1.

A. C. Newby, *Training Evaluation Handbook*. Gower, Aldershot, 1992.

John W. Newston and Edward E. Scannel, *Games Trainers Play. Experiential Learning Exercises*. McGraw-Hill, San Francisco, 1980.

I. MacKay, *A Guide to Listening*, 2nd impression. British Association for Commercial and Industrial Education, London, 1990.

G. Pask and B. Lewis, *Teaching Strategies: A Systems Approach*. Open University Press, Milton Keynes, 1972.

Allan Pease, *Body Language. How to Read Others' Thoughts by their Gestures*. Sheldon Press, London, 1981.

J. W. Pfeiffer and J. G. Jones (eds), *The Annual Handbook for Group Facilitators* (19 vols). University Associates, San Diego, California, 1972–95.

J. Phillips, *Handbook of Training Evaluation and Measurement Methods* (2nd edn). Kogan Page, London, 1991.

M. Picciotto, I. Robertson and R. Colley, *Interactivity: Designing and Using Interactive Video*. Kogan Page, London, 1989.

P. R. Pinto and J. W. Walker, *A Study of Training Development Roles and Competencies*. American Society for Training & Development, Washington, D. C., 1978.

T. Pont, *Investing in Training and Development: Turning Interest Into Capital*. Kogan Page, London, 1995.

L. S. Powell, *A Guide to the Overhead Projector*. BACIE, London, 1964.

L. S. Powell, *A Guide to the Use of Visual Aids*. BACIE, London, 1978.

P. Race, *The Open Learning Handbook. Selecting, Designing, and Supporting Open Learning Materials*. Kogan Page, London, 1989.

L. Rae, *The Skills of Training. A Guide for Managers and Practitioners*. Gower, Aldershot, 1983.

D. Reay, *Evaluating Training*. Kogan Page, London, 1994.

M. A. Reid, H. Barrington and J. Kenney, *Training Interventions: managing employee development* (3rd edn). Institute of Personnel Management, London, 1992.

R. W. Revans, *Developing Effective Managers*. Longman, Harlow, 1971.

R. W. Revans, *The Origins and Growth of Action Learning*. Chartwell Bratt, Bromley, 1982.

R. W. Revans, *ABC of Action Learning*. Chartwell Bratt, Bromley, 1983.

M. Robson, *Facilitating*. Gower, Aldershot, 1995.

C. Rogers, *Freedom to Learn*. Merrill, Columbus, Ohio, 1983.

A. J. Romiszowski, *The Selection and Use of Instructional Media. For Improved Classroom Teaching and for Interactive Individualised Instruction* (2nd edn). Kogan Page, London, 1988.

D. Rowntree, *Exploring Open and Distance Learning*. Kogan Page, London, 1992.

T. Russell, *Effective Feedback Skills*. Kogan Page, London, 1994.

J. Schwab, M. Baldwin, J. Gerber, M. Gomori and V. Satir, *The Satir Approach to Communication: A Workshop Leaders Manual*. Science and Behaviour Books, Palo Alto, California, 1989.

M. E. Shaw, R. J. Corsini, R. Blake and S. Mouton, *Role Playing: A Practical Manual for Group Facilitators*. University Associates, San Diego, California, 1980.

B. F. Skinner, *Science & Human Behaviour*. Macmillan, New York, 1953.

B. F. Skinner, *Beyond Freedom & Dignity*. Knopf, New York, 1971.

T. Spinks and P. Clements, *A Practical Guide to Facilitation Skills. A Real World Approach*. Kogan Page, London, 1993.

B. Tate, *Open Learning Choices for Managers*. Gower, Aldershot, 1995.

A. Tough, *The Adults' Learning Projects. A Fresh Approach to Theory and Practice* (2nd edn). The Ontario Institute for Studies in Education, Toronto, Ontario, 1979.

Lao Tzu, *The Way of Life* (trans. Witter Bynner). Perigee Books, New York, 1980.

University Associates, *Encyclopedia of Icebreakers*. San Diego, California, 1983.

V. H. Vroom, *Work and Motivation*. Wiley, New York, 1964.

P. Warr, M. Bird and N. Rackham, *Evaluation of Management Training*. Gower, Aldershot, 1970.

J. N. Wismer, 'Communication effectiveness: active listening and sending feeling messages', in *The Annual Handbook for Group Facilitators* (J. W. Pfeiffer and J. E. Jones, eds). University Associates, San Diego, California, 1978.

R. M. Yerkes and J. D. Dodson, 'The relation of strength of stimulus to rapidity of habit formation', *J. Comp. Neurol. Psychol.* **18** (1908), 459–82.

A. Zander, *Groups At Work*. Jossey Bass, San Francisco, 1977.

Index

Further titles in the McGraw-Hill Training Series

WORKSHOPS THAT WORK
100 Ideas to Make Your Training Events More Effective
Tom Bourner, Vivien Martin, Phil Race
ISBN 0-07-707800-4

THE HANDBOOK FOR ORGANIZATIONAL CHANGE
Strategy and Skill for Trainers and Developers
Carol A. O'Connor
ISBN 0-07-707693-1

TRAINING FOR PROFIT
A Guide to the Integration of Training in an Organization's
Success
Philip Darling
ISBN 0-07-707786-5

TEAM BUILDING
A Practical Guide for Trainers
Neil Clark
ISBN 0-07-707846-2

DEVELOPING MANAGERS AS COACHES
A Trainer's Guide
Frank Salisbury
ISBN 0-07-707892-6

THE ASSERTIVE TRAINER
A Practical Guide for Trainers
Liz Willis and Jenny Daisley
ISBN 0-07-707077-2

MEETING MANAGEMENT
A Manual of Effective Training Material
Leslie Rae
ISBN 0-07-707782-2

LEARNING THROUGH SIMULATIONS
A Guide to the Design and Use of Simulations in Business and
Education
John Fripp
ISBN 0-07-707588-9 paperback
ISBN 0-07-707789-X Disk

IMAGINATIVE EVENTS Volumes I & II
A Sourcebook of Innovative Simulations, Exercises, Puzzles
and Games
Ken Jones
ISBN 0-07-707679-6 Volume I
ISBN 0-07-707680-X Volume II
ISBN 0-07-707681-8 Set Ringbinder

TRAINING TO MEET THE TECHNOLOGY CHALLENGE
Trevor Bentley
ISBN 0-07-707589-7

CLIENT-CENTRED CONSULTING
A Practical Guide for Internal Advisers and Trainers
Peter Cockman, Bill Evans and Peter Reynolds
ISBN 0-07-707685-0

TOTAL QUALITY TRAINING
The Quality Culture and Quality Trainer
Brian Thomas
ISBN 0-07-707472-6

CAREER DEVELOPMENT AND PLANNING
A Guide for Managers, Trainers and Personnel Staff
Malcolm Peel
ISBN 0-07-707554-4

DESIGNING AND ACHIEVING COMPETENCY
A Competency-based Approach to Developing People and
Organizations
Edited by Rosemary Boam and Paul Sparrow
ISBN 0-07-707572-2

SELF-DEVELOPMENT
A Facilitator's Guide
Mike Pedler and David Megginson
ISBN 0-07-707460-2

DEVELOPING WOMEN THROUGH TRAINING
A Practical Handbook
Liz Willis and Jenny Daisley
ISBN 0-07-707566-8

HOW TO SUCCEED IN EMPLOYEE DEVELOPMENT
Moving from Vision to Results
Ed Moorby
ISBN 0-07-707459-9

MAKING MANAGEMENT DEVELOPMENT WORK
Achieving Success in the Nineties
Charles Margerison
ISBN 0-07-707382-7

MANAGING PERSONAL LEARNING AND CHANGE
A Trainer's Guide
Neil Clark
ISBN 0-07-707344-4

THE BUSINESS OF TRAINING
Achieving Success in Changing World Markets
Trevor Bentley
ISBN 0-07-707328-2

All books are published by:

McGraw-Hill Book Company Europe
Shoppenhangers Road, Maidenhead, Berkshire SL6 2QL, England
Tel: (01628) 23432   Fax: (01628) 770224